TOP 10

DEVON & CORNWALL

ROBERT ANDREWS

DK

EYEWITNESS TRAVEL

Left **The Harbour Hotel, Newquay** Centre **Ottery St Mary** Right **Circular houses in Veryan**

LONDON, NEW YORK,
MELBOURNE, MUNICH AND DELHI
www.dk.com

Design, Editorial and Picture Research by
Quadrum Solutions, Krishnamai, 33B, Sir
Pochkhanwala Road, Worli, Mumbai, India

Printed and bound in China

First published in the UK in 2009 by Dorling
Kindersley Limited, 80 Strand, London
WC2R 0RL
A Penguin Random House Company

14 15 16 17 10 9 8 7 6 5 4 3 2 1

**Copyright 2009, 2015 © Dorling
Kindersley Limited, London**

Reprinted with revisions 2011, 2013, 2015

A CIP catalogue record is available from the
British Library.

ISBN 978-1-4093-7008-6

Within each Top 10 list in this book, no
hierarchy of quality or popularity is implied.
All 10 are, in the editor's opinion,

Contents

Devon and Cornwall's Top 10

Cover: Front – **Robert Harding Picture Library**: Adam Burton c; **Alamy Images**: Justin Kase z02z bl.
Spine – **DK Images**: Kim Sayer b. Back – **DK Images**: Nigel Hicks tl, tr; Kim Sayer tc.

Left **Porthminster Beach, St Ives** Right **The Italianate Garden, Mount Edgcumbe**

Left **Padstow Harbour** Right **Powderham Castle**

Key to abbreviations
Adm admission charge

DEVON AND CORNWALL'S TOP 10

DEVON AND CORNWALL'S TOP 10

TOP10 Devon and Cornwall's Highlights

The Southwest peninsula holds some of Britain's most forbidding moorland, dramatic coastline and enticing beaches. Its history, stretching from Celtic to Victorian times, is strikingly illustrated in its castles and stately homes, while year-round, a range of outdoor activities and all-weather attractions provide entertainment and instruction for the whole family. Equally renowned for old-fashioned tranquillity and soul-stirring views, Devon and Cornwall provide the ideal canvas for the perfect holiday.

1 Lanhydrock
This impressive 17th-century mansion is filled with Jacobean art and Victorian furnishings. Immaculate gardens and sweeping parkland surround the house *(see pp8–9)*.

2 Eden Project
Conservation is made fun at this wide-ranging exploration of the plant world, dominated by two giant greenhouses. Summer concerts, winter ice-skating and several cafés and restaurants serving great food enhance its appeal *(see pp10–11)*.

3 Dartmoor
A range of activities is possible on this bleak expanse of moorland, which is complemented by grand houses and cosy villages sheltering thatched pubs *(see pp12–13)*.

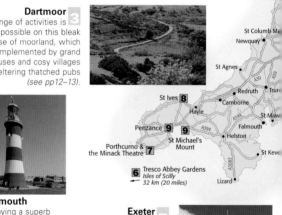

Padstow

St Columb Ma

Newquay

St Agnes

A30

Redruth · Truro

St Ives 8

Camborne

Hayle

St Maw

Penzance 9 9

A394

Falmouth

Porthcurno & 7
the Minack Theatre

St Michael's
Mount

Helston

St Keve

6 Tresco Abbey Gardens
Isles of Scilly
← 32 km (20 miles)

Lizard

4 Plymouth
Enjoying a superb location, this seafaring city was the home port of the intrepid sailor Sir Francis Drake. It still preserves traces of the Elizabethan era. Within a short distance are palatial houses and country parks *(see pp14–15)*.

5 Exeter
Rising from the River Exe, the capital of Devon has a strong historical flavour, not least in its cathedral and other ancient monuments. It also has a buzzing and vibrant contemporary cultural life *(see pp18–21)*.

Preceding pages **A biome at the Eden Project**

7 Porthcurno and the Minack Theatre

Porthcurno has a range of outdoor attractions, including a sandy beach between high cliffs and the open-air Minack Theatre, hewn out of the rock *(see pp24–5)*.

6 Tresco Abbey Gardens

On a wind-blasted island in the middle of the Atlantic, this gracious garden of semi-tropical plants has been created within the walls of a ruined abbey *(see pp22–3)*.

8 St Ives

Home to the Tate St Ives gallery, this quirky seaside town has a thriving arts scene. Sandy beaches and excellent restaurants are further attractions here *(see pp26–7)*.

9 Penzance and St Michael's Mount

The region's most westerly town is home to two superb galleries and is close to St Michael's Mount, a fortified house crowning an island *(see pp28–9)*.

10 Padstow

Famous for its gourmet restaurants, this North Cornwall fishing port is also notable for its beaches, historic houses and a cycling and walking trail *(see pp30–31)*.

Check out www.visitcornwall.com and www.visitdevon.co.uk.

Top 10 Lanhydrock

This magnificent 17th-century mansion set in the Fowey Valley is one of England's grandest country houses. Built originally by a rich merchant, Sir Richard Robartes, it remained in the same family until the National Trust took it over in 1953. It was reconstructed in 1881 following a disastrous fire. Though parts of the Jacobean building survived – notably its famous Long Gallery – the dominant style is that of the High Victorian era. The warren of 50 visitable rooms offers a glimpse into life inside a stately pile, from the huge kitchens to Lady Robartes' boudoir.

1 Captain Tommy's Bedroom

This room is dedicated to Thomas Agar-Robartes, who died in the Battle of Loos in 1915. A suitcase kept on the cast-iron bed contains his personal items.

The gardens at Lanhydrock

⏲ Enjoy the great view from the stairs of the Gatehouse. Free tours of the gardens are organized from here everyday.

🍴 In the house, the Servants' Hall restaurant offers food, and there is a snack bar in the stables.

- Map D4
- Near Bodmin, Cornwall
- 01208 265950
- House: open Apr–Sep: 11am–5:30pm Tue–Sun & national hols; Mar & Oct: 11am–5pm Tue–Sun; garden: open mid-Feb–Oct 10am–6pm daily
- Adm £11.30, child £5.65, family £16.95; grounds £7, child £3.50
- www.nationaltrust.org.uk

Top 10 Features

1. Captain Tommy's Bedroom
2. Woodland Walks
3. The Gardens
4. The Gatehouse
5. The Dining Room
6. The Billiard Room
7. The Nursery Wing
8. The Kitchen
9. The Long Gallery
10. St Hydroc Church

2 Woodland Walks

The woods and parkland of the estate are lovely to explore. Here, you can enjoy the exuberant birdlife and, in spring, brilliant expanses of bluebells *(above)* and daffodils.

3 The Gardens

The clipped yew trees and geometric flower-beds are striking *(below)*, but it is the magnolias in the shrub garden for which the gardens are most renowned.

Discounts are offered to visitors who arrive by bicycle or public transport.

The Gatehouse
This impressive, pinnacled structure was built in around 1650. The main room on the upper storey was used to entertain ladies while the men hunted. It leads into the Topiary Courtyard.

The Dining Room
Decorated with blue-and-gilt wallpaper designed by William Morris, the dining room is dominated by a table set for a formal meal as it would have been in Victorian times.

The Billiard Room
This spacious room exudes the spirit of the leisured life of the gentry with its billiard table *(above)* and tiger skin set against oak-panelling. Old school photos and other mementos line the walls.

The Nursery Wing
A whole suite of rooms was set aside for bringing up the younger family members. The nursery itself is crowded with a large doll's house and rocking horse among other toys *(above)*.

The Kitchen
At the heart of the building is the main kitchen where the cook and servants worked. The vast interior resembles a church with its rafters and gabled roof.

The Long Gallery
Lanhydrock's *pièce de résistance* occupying the north wing's entire first floor, is famed for its remarkable plaster ceiling which illustrates stories from the Old Testament.

Below Stairs
More than any other house of its period, Lanhydrock provides an intriguing insight into how a grand mansion actually operated. Passages lead from the main kitchen, with its elaborate ranges and gleaming copper, to sculleries, larders, a bakehouse and a dairy. At the top of the house are the nurseries and the modest servants' quarters, which are a stark contrast to the lavish bedrooms of the owners.

St Hydroc Church
Dedicated to an Irish missionary, the church *(right)*, adjoining the house, dates from the 15th century. A plaster panel in the north aisle displays the arms of King James I, dated 1621.

Bikes can be hired to explore off-road cycle trails through the grounds.

🔟 Eden Project

A china clay pit transformed to house two giant conservatories and an extensive area of outdoor beds, the Eden Project is an innovative exploration of the plant world and man's interaction with it. Although it is the grand spectacle of the place that grabs the attention, the Eden Project has a serious agenda, aimed at alerting us to the fragility of Earth's ecosystem, through talks and workshops organized around the year. The educational element, however, does not stifle the sense of fun. In summer, this is one of the region's best venues for open-air concerts, while the arena becomes an ice rink in winter.

An orchid at the Rainforest Biome

Outdoor seating at one of Eden's cafés

🕐 Eden can be taxing on the feet, but the Land Train provides some relief – especially for the ascent to the exit.

🍴 There is no need to bring food here – Eden has many good-quality restaurants and cafés.

• Map D4
• Bodelva, Cornwall
• 01726 811911
• Open Apr–Oct: 9:30am–6pm daily; Aug: closes 8pm Mon, Tue, Wed & Thu; Nov–mid-Mar: 10am–4:30pm; last adm 90 min before closing
• Adm £23.50, child £13.50, seniors & students £18.50; reduced prices for tickets booked online.
• www.edenproject. com

Top 10 Features

1. Visitor Centre
2. Rainforest Biome
3. Mediterranean Biome
4. Eden Sessions
5. Eden's Restaurants
6. The Spiral Garden
7. Eden's Artworks
8. Outside Biome
9. The Core
10. The Canopy Walkway

1 Visitor Centre

Adorned with sculptures, such as Heather Jansch's *Driftwood Horse* made from driftwood and cork, the Visitor Centre, a lofty viewpoint at the top of the pit, gives a taste of the marvels to come. From here, the full scale of the place becomes apparent.

Mediterranean Biome 3

The smaller of the two indoor biomes *(right)* houses plants from the Mediterranean, South Africa and southwestern America. Exhibits include orange trees, olives and vividly coloured flowers.

2 Rainforest Biome

Hot and steamy with a waterfall coursing through it, this luxuriant biome *(left)* recreates a tropical climate for plants and rainforest flowers from West Africa, Amazonia and Malaysia.

Those who don't arrive by car are offered a substantial discount.

4 Eden Sessions

The crowd-pulling "Eden Sessions" held in summer have included memorable gigs by Ellie Goulding, Calvin Harris, Kaiser Chiefs *(above)* and lesser-known artists.

5 Eden's Restaurants

The award-winning restaurants here offer global cuisine prepared with locally sourced ingredients. Dishes include everything from enchiladas to char-grilled halloumi cheese and even Cornish cream tea. Restaurants include the Apple Café, Jo's Café and the Bakery.

6 The Spiral Garden

This innovative garden, designed with children in mind, explores patterns in nature and allows visitors to touch plants, roll on the grass and clamber through tunnels.

7 Eden's Artworks

The artworks at Eden include specially commissioned temporary exhibits and permanent displays, such as a giant bee *(below)* and Dionysian figures in the Mediterranean Biome.

8 Outside Biome

In this roofless biome, plants are cultivated in Cornwall's temperate climate. Native Cornish flora is found alongside plants from Australasia and Chile.

9 The Core

The message of the Eden Project – mankind's dependence on Earth's resources – is presented with flair at the Core, an education centre and exhibition venue. The building's design mimics that of a tree. Its centrepiece is *Seed (left)*, a granite sculpture by artist Peter Randall-Page.

10 The Canopy Walkway

Set high above the tree tops in the Rainforest Biome, this offers a bird's eye view, with the stunning biodiversity chandelier overhead.

Eden – Facts and Figures

Nearly 60 m (200 ft) deep, the former china clay pit required 85,000 tonnes of soil (a mix of china clay and composted waste) to transform it into a horticultural wonderland. The site contains over a million plants of more than 5,000 species. Based on designs by architect R B Fuller, Eden's covered biomes are the world's largest conservatories – the 50-m (164-ft) high Rainforest Biome could hold the Tower of London.

Between October and February, the arena is iced over to provide a spectacular skating rink.

TOP 10 Dartmoor

Southern England's greatest expanse of wilderness holds a unique fascination, its heather-strewn slopes and rocky tors haunted by legends and scattered with relics of the people who inhabited it 3,000 years ago. Hemmed in by the moorland are some of Devon's grandest mansions, its comeliest villages and its most enticing pubs. The main towns of Okehampton and Tavistock hold markets and museums, while Princetown, at the centre of the moor, has the main information facilities, where you can find out about organized walks on a network of footpaths that give access to the remotest areas. There is also plenty of scope for cycling and riding, and more adventurous pursuits such as caving, canoeing, climbing and nature safaris.

The Dartmoor Inn

🍴 In Lydford, the Castle Inn provides food and drink. Book ahead for the more refined fare of the Dartmoor Inn, *(see p81).*

- Map J4
- Okehampton Castle: Glendale Rd, Okehampton; 01837 52844; adm £4, child £2.40; www.english-heritage.org.uk
- Castle Drogo: Drewsteignton; 01647 433306; castle: adm £8.70, child £4.30, family £21.80; Grounds: adm £5.50, child £3
- Museum of Dartmoor Life: 3 West St, Okehampton; 01837 52295; open Apr–mid-Dec: 10:15am–4:15pm Mon–Fri, 10:15am–1pm Sat; adm £2.50; www.museum ofdartmoorlife.org.uk
- Lydford Gorge: The Stables, Lydford; 01822 820320; in winter access restricted to main waterfall & top of gorge; adm £6.90, child £3.40, family £10.30

Top 10 Features

1. Okehampton Castle
2. Castle Drogo
3. Grimspound
4. Museum of Dartmoor Life
5. Dartmeet
6. Widecombe-in-the-Moor
7. Fingle Bridge
8. Lydford Gorge
9. Merrivale Rows
10. Wistman's Wood

1 Okehampton Castle

A tall, seemingly tottering tower greets you as you approach this ancient Norman construction *(above)* surrounded by woodland. Inside, you can view the remains of the gatehouse, keep and Great Hall.

2 Castle Drogo

Said to be the last castle built in England, this formidable building was constructed in the early 20th century by architect Edwin Lutyens on the whim of grocery magnate Julius Drewe. The lush grounds lead down to the River Teign.

3 Grimspound

To the north of Widecombe, these circular prehistoric huts surrounded by a thick wall *(left)* are said to have been the model for the Stone Age village where Sherlock Holmes camped in the novel, *The Hound of the Baskervilles.*

Call the sights listed in the panel on the left to check opening times.

Museum of Dartmoor Life
This museum *(above)* provides a fascinating insight into the lives of the moor's inhabitants, past and present. Displays include everything from antique agricultural tools and farm pick-ups to domestic bric-a-brac.

Map showing Dartmoor National Park with locations: Okehampton, Meldon, Lydford, Tavistock, Drewsteignton, Moretonhampstead, Bovey Tracey, Postbridge, Two Bridges, Princetown, Dartmeet, Widecombe-in-the-Moor, Ashburton, Yelverton, Buckfastleigh

Dartmeet
This is a renowned beauty spot at the junction of the East and West Dart rivers. Nearby is one of Dartmoor's famous clapper bridges *(centre)* – ancient crossing points.

Widecombe-in-the-Moor
This idyllic village is known for its pinnacled church tower *(above)* – a prominent landmark – and for the famous folk ditty, *Widdicombe Fair*.

Fingle Bridge
Crowds home in on this bridge over the River Teign, but you can find peace on the paths that weave along the shaded banks. The Fingle Bridge Inn provides snacks.

Lydford Gorge
In this remote ravine, the River Lyd tumbles over the 30-m (100-ft) White Lady Waterfall *(above)* and through dense vegetation that shelters wildlife.

Merrivale Rows
Trailing across moorland west of Princetown, these stones give an idea of the kind of prehistoric society that lived here. The complex includes huts and granite tombs.

Wistman's Wood
A couple of miles from the road near Two Bridges, this tangled wood is a remnant of the time when the moor was fully forested. The ancient, mossy trunks create a fine setting for a picnic.

The Hound of the Baskervilles

This Conan Doyle yarn may have had various possible sources. Local myths tell of a huntsman who terrorized the countryside accompanied by a pack of red-eyed hounds. Another inspiration may have been the legend of the Black Dog of Dartmoor who, it is said, chased late-night travellers on the coach road all the way to their destination.

Plymouth

Devon's largest conurbation, and one of Britain's greatest seafaring cities, Plymouth produced such seadogs as Francis Drake and John Hawkins, both of whom played a leading role in the rout of the Spanish Armada in 1588. An important naval base, the city endured ferocious bombing in World War II and fared little better from insensitive rebuilding in the war's aftermath. Fortunately, its historic Barbican district and adjacent harbour have survived intact, along with a handful of timber-framed and jettied historic buildings. Added to these are some compelling modern attractions and a lively cultural scene, all of which repay a visit to this old harbour city.

Monuments on the Hoe

🔵 **At the top of Black Friars Distillery, the Barbican Kitchen is perfect for a meal.**

• *National Marine Aquarium: map Q6; Coxside; 08448 937938; adm £13.75*
• *Saltram: map N5; Plympton; 01752 333500; adm £10, garden adm £5.10*
• *Mount Edgcumbe: Cremyll, Torpoint; 01752 822236; adm £7.20*
• *City Museum and Art Gallery: map Q4; Drake Circus; 01752 304774; adm free*
• *Mayflower Exhibition: 3–5 The Barbican; 01752 306330; adm £2*
• *Merchant's House Museum: map P5; 33 St Andrew's St; 01752 304774; adm £2.60*
• *Black Friars Distillery: map P5; 60 Southside St; 01752 665292; adm £7*
• *Elizabethan House: map Q5; 32 New St; 01752 304774; adm £2.60*

Top 10 Features

1. Plymouth Hoe
2. National Marine Aquarium
3. Saltram
4. Mount Edgcumbe
5. City Museum and Art Gallery
6. Mayflower Exhibition
7. Merchant's House Museum
8. Black Friars Distillery
9. Sutton Harbour
10. Elizabethan House

Plymouth Hoe

High above the harbour looking out over Plymouth Sound, the Hoe is a grassy expanse studded with memorials and a relocated lighthouse – Smeaton's Tower *(centre)*. Lawns and flowerbeds make this an ideal spot in fine weather.

National Marine Aquarium

Plymouth's most high-profile attraction *(below)* features a range of marine life, such as sharks, moray eels and seahorses. Panels provide insights into life under-water. Feeding times take place throughout the day.

Saltram

An elegant Georgian mansion set in its own grounds outside Plymouth, Saltram is adorned with exquisite furnishings *(above)* and works of art. Several scenes in the film *Sense and Sensibility* were shot here.

4 Mount Edgcumbe

Set on the Rame Peninsula facing Plymouth across the Sound, Mount Edgcumbe *(above)* is surrounded by parkland that offers stupendous views of the city and along the coast.

5 City Museum and Art Gallery

The wide-ranging exhibits here include Egyptian statuettes, porcelain, portraits by Joshua Reynolds and local archaeological finds.

6 Mayflower Exhibition

This extensive exhibition provides a fascinating insight into seafaring adventures, including the epic voyage of the Pilgrim Fathers to the New World.

7 Merchant's House Museum

This 17th-century building *(above)* houses a collection of curiosities including a ducking stool, a huge Victorian doll's house, a pharmacy and a reconstructed schoolroom.

8 Black Friars Distillery

Originally a merchant's house, this distillery has been producing Plymouth Gin since 1793. It is believed that the Pilgrim Fathers sought shelter here before journeying on the *Mayflower*.

9 Sutton Harbour

The harbour *(below)* was the embarkation point for Captain Cook, and, earlier in 1620, for the Pilgrim Fathers as marked by the Mayflower Steps and a plaque.

10 Elizabethan House

This Tudor home preserves its low ceilings and creaking oak floors. A restored kitchen is on the ground floor, the dining room and parlour on the first floor and bedrooms on the second.

The Historical Port

Formerly a small fishing community, Plymouth prospered in the 15th and 16th centuries as a naval base and a port for wool shipments. The Pilgrim Fathers embarked from here in 1620 to found the American colony of New Plymouth. Captain Cook and Charles Darwin both sailed from here in later centuries. The city's naval presence continues to be strong.

Call the sights to check opening times and tours.

Left **The Citadel** Centre **Bowling Green Hotel** Right **Memorial to the Spanish Armada**

☆10 The Plymouth Hoe

1 Drake's Statue
This statue of Drake gazes grandly over the Sound. His cutlass and globe represent his circumnavigation of the world. ✪ Map P6

2 Smeaton's Tower
Originally built in 1759 on Eddystone Rocks miles out to sea, the top half of this lighthouse was rebuilt on the Hoe in 1882. A popular attraction, it affords lofty sea views. ✪ Map P6 • 01752 304774 • Open Apr–Sep: 10am–4:30pm daily; Oct, Nov, Feb & Mar: 10am–3pm Tue–Sat • Adm • www. plymouth.gov.uk

Smeaton's Tower

3 Naval Memorial
This obelisk commemorates more than 23,000 dead and missing sailors from Plymouth and other Commonwealth nations in the two world wars. ✪ Map P6

4 Tinside Lido
This elegant outdoor pool is located right next to the sea and below the Hoe. It is the perfect place for lounging and relaxing. Built in 1935, it is not heated, but the sheer Art Deco exuberance compensates for any chill. ✪ Map P6 • Hoe Road • 01752 261915 • Open late May–late Jul: noon–6pm Mon–Fri, 10am–6pm Sat & Sun; late Jul–early Sep: 10am–6pm daily except 7:30pm Wed • www. everyoneactive.com

5 City of Plymouth Bowling Club
Sir Francis Drake is believed to have insisted on finishing his game of bowls at this club on the Hoe before sailing to meet the Spanish Armada. ✪ Map P6 • Lockyer Street • Open late Apr–Sep • 01752 339920

6 The Promenade
Enjoy the distant views, tidy lawns and the pretty flowerbeds from this broad promenade running across the Hoe. ✪ Map P6

7 Royal Citadel
Towering over the quayside at the base of the Hoe, this sturdy fortress was built in 1666 and is

The waterfront at the Hoe

Top 10 Events in Drake's Life

1. Born in Tavistock, Dartmoor, around 1540.
2. Apprenticed to a coastal vessel around 1553.
3. Enlists in the fleet of the Hawkins family in 1563.
4. In 1572, becomes the first Englishman to sight the Pacific.
5. Becomes the first Englishman to circumnavigate the world, 1577–80. Knighted by Queen Elizabeth.
6. Made Mayor of Plymouth, 1581. Moves into Buckland Abbey.
7. Plunders Spain's American possessions in command of a fleet of 25 ships in 1585.
8. Raids Cadiz and delays the Spanish invasion fleet of Philip II by a year.
9. Plays a leading part in defeating the Spanish Armada in 1588.
10. Dies of fever in the West Indies in 1596.

Sir Francis Drake

The most renowned seaman of the Elizabethan Age and one of the world's greatest sailors, Francis Drake won fame and fortune on his raids against the Spanish Main. With his exploits, not least his circumnavigation of the globe and his subsequent role in defeating the Spanish Armada, he embodied many of the virtues of expansionist Elizabethan England. He achieved official recognition when he was knighted by the queen. Though he also participated in the slave trade, his seamanship and military skill made him a national hero.

A statue of Sir Francis Drake

still a military base. Visitors can tour the ramparts, St Katherine's Chapel and the Governor's House. ◈ Map P6–Q6
• Guided tours: May–Sep 2:30pm Tue & Thu; prior booking not required • Adm
• www.english-heritage.org.uk

Memorial to the Spanish Armada

This memorial dates from 1890 and is surmounted by a bronze figure of Britannia. The shields on the base show the arms of the towns that contributed men, money and ships to the English fleet. ◈ Map P6

Air Force Memorial

Topped by a bare-headed pilot, this memorial records the huge losses suffered by the Royal Air Force in World War II, mostly from Bomber Command. Commonwealth and Allied losses are also remembered. ◈ Map N6

The View

The magnificent panorama from the Hoe extends over Plymouth Sound – the sheltered estuary basin – embracing Drake's Island, the breakwater and usually a flotilla of sailing vessels. ◈ Map P6–N6

⁸⁄₁₀ Exeter

Rising up from the River Exe and dominated by the twin towers of its cathedral, Exeter holds more historical interest than any other city in the region. The days when it was a byword for provincial respectability are long gone and Exeter now has a vibrant cultural life, enlivened by students from its university and enhanced by the splendid Royal Albert Memorial Museum. Its compact centre is easy to negotiate on foot, while the Quay is a pleasant spot to sit and have a snack. In the evening, pick from one of the city's many restaurants or visit its historic pubs.

The Quay

🍴 Eat at outdoor tables at On the Waterfront, a 19th-century warehouse on the Quay.

• *Tourist office: map Q2; Dix's Field, Paris St; 01392 665700; www. exeter.gov.uk*
• *Exeter Cathedral: map Q2; Cathedral Close; 01392 285983; open 9am–4:45pm daily; adm £6, students & senior citizens £4; www.exeter-cathedral.org.uk*
• *The Guildhall: map P2; High St; 01392 665500*
• *Bill Douglas Cinema Museum: map P2; University of Exeter, The Old Library, Prince of Wales Rd; 01392 724321; www.bdcmuseum.org.uk*
• *Underground Passages: map Q2; 2 Paris St; 01392 665887; adm £6, child (5–18) £4*
• *St Nicholas Priory: map P2; The Mint, off Fore St; 01392 271732; adm £4.20*
• *Royal Albert Memorial Museum: map P2; Queen St, 01392 265858; open 10am–5pm Tue–Sun; adm free; www. rammuseum.org.uk*

Top 10 Features

1. Exeter Cathedral
2. The Quay
3. Stepcote Hill
4. The Guildhall
5. Bill Douglas Cinema Museum
6. Underground Passages
7. St Nicholas Priory
8. Along the Exe
9. Quay House
10. Royal Albert Memorial Museum

¹ Exeter Cathedral

Sheltered within the harmonious Close, the cathedral's most compelling features lie in its 14th-century Gothic style, notably its carved, honey-coloured façade *(centre)* and its vaulted nave – the longest in the country.

² The Quay

Once a hard-working harbour, the Quay *(above)* now offers peace and quiet by day, with only a few cafés and crafts and antiques shops. In contrast, the evenings can be lively, with pubs and clubs drawing in the crowds.

³ Stepcote Hill

This steep, medieval lane was once a busy main route into town. Tudor buildings *(below)* stand at the bottom alongside one of Exeter's oldest churches, St Mary Steps.

For opening times and other information, call the sights or check their websites.

The Guildhall
Dating from 1330, this building *(above)* still serves municipal functions but you can pop in to admire the portraits in the main chamber.

Bill Douglas Cinema Museum
Cinematic memorabilia is displayed in this centre located on the university campus. Exhibits range from early movie cameras and Charlie Chaplin posters to Shirley Temple dolls and *E.T.* money boxes.

Underground Passages
This subterranean network was built in the 14th century to carry water into the city. Guided tours through the tunnels are fascinating.

St Nicholas Priory
This Benedictine priory survived the Dissolution of the Monasteries. Medieval household objects *(above)* are displayed on the first floor.

Along the Exe
Enjoy a tranquil walk or cycle ride along the Exeter Ship Canal and the Exe Estuary, and spot a range of birdlife along the way. Bikes can be hired from the Quay.

Quay House
This restored 17th-century building on the Quay now houses a visitor centre with an audiovisual exhibition of the city's history, as well as models and paintings.

Royal Albert Memorial Museum
Apart from a fine art collection, this Victorian Neo-Gothic building has numerous evocative displays on world cultures, local and natural history, costumes and textiles.

Exeter's Festivals
The Vibraphonic Festival in March brings big names in the world of jazz, funk and soul to the city, while local gastronomy is celebrated in the Exeter Festival of South West Food & Drink (March/April), which includes cooking demonstrations by master-chefs and activities for kids. Exeter Respect Festival (end of May) and Unexpected Exeter (August) feature local artists.

Left **Buildings on Cathedral Close** Right **Stained-glass windows adorning the cathedral**

Exeter Cathedral

1 Gothic Façade
Apostles, prophets and soldiers jostle for space on the crowded carved West Front of the cathedral. Also look out for the kings Alfred, Athelstan, Canute, William I and Richard II.

2 Ceiling
This is the longest unbroken Gothic ceiling in the world. It makes an immediate impression with a dense network of rib-vaulting, shafts and mouldings. One of the ceiling bosses shows the murder of Thomas à Becket, Archbishop of Canterbury, in 1170.

3 Minstrels' Gallery
High up on the left side of the nave is a minstrels' gallery, which was built in 1350. It depicts 12 angels playing musical instruments.

4 Sepulchre of Hugh Courtenay
The cathedral is crammed with tombs, none more eye-catching than the 14th-century sepulchre of Hugh Courtenay, Earl of Devon, and his wife. Their tomb is carved with graceful swans and a lion.

5 Chapter House
From the right transept, a door leads into the Chapter House, originally constructed in the 1220s but mostly rebuilt after a fire in 1413. Beneath the fine timber ceiling stands an array of sculptures from the 20th century. The Chapter House is also a venue for classical music concerts. You can pick up a leaflet for details.

The Exeter Clock

6 Exeter Clock
The clock in the left transept dates from the late 15th century, though the minutes dial was added only in 1759. The sun and moon revolve round the Earth, in the form of a golden ball.

7 Choir
Dominated by a 18-m (60-ft) bishop's throne and a massive organ case, the Choir (or "Quire") holds stalls dating from the 19th century, but with carvings that date from as far back as the 1250s, one showing an elephant.

The Minstrels' Gallery

Top 10 Key Events in Exeter's History

1. Exeter is fortified by the Romans in AD 50–55.
2. Around 878, the city is re-founded by Alfred the Great.
3. In 1068, the Normans take control and expand the wool trade.
4. The countess of Devon diverts the shipping trade to Topsham in the late 13th century.
5. In 1369, work is completed on Exeter Cathedral.
6. In 1564–66, the Quay and the Ship Canal are constructed.
7. The city shelters Charles I's queen in 1643, but falls to the Roundheads in 1646.
8. Trade ceases during the Napoleonic wars (1800–15), damaging the local textile industry.
9. World War II bombing flattens the city centre.
10. In 2007, the Princesshay development spearheads a regeneration of the historic centre.

Cannon outside Custom House on the Quay

Exeter's History

Previously a settlement of the Celtic Dumnonii tribe, Exeter became the most westerly outpost of the Roman Empire in Britain when it was garrisoned in around AD 50–55. Saxon settlement was followed by Danish attacks, but conditions were peaceful under the Norman regime after 1068. Exeter's position on the River Exe allowed it to become a major outlet for wool shipments. During the Civil War, it became the western headquarters of the Royalists and sheltered Charles I's queen. In the 20th century, bombing during World War II spared the cathedral, but devastated the historic centre. However, the founding of the University of Exeter in 1955 helped inject new energy into the city, and the Princesshay development has since reversed some of the damage done by shabby postwar reconstruction.

Plaque to R D Blackmore
8 Among the tombs and memorials that line the walls of the aisles is one near the door, which is dedicated to R D Blackmore *(see p56)*, author of the rip-roaring Exmoor tale, *Lorna Doone*.

Cathedral Close
9 The lawns surrounding the cathedral are a pleasant place to relax. They are over-looked by an array of historical buildings, including the splendid Elizabethan Mol's Coffee House, which is now a shoe shop. The remains of a Roman bath house and a Saxon burial site lie beneath the lawns.

The Towers
10 Dating from the 12th century, the two central towers are the oldest part of the cathedral. They are still the most conspicuous feature of Exeter's skyline.

TOP 10 Tresco Abbey Gardens

Like a cross between Kew Gardens and the Amazonian jungle, Tresco Abbey Gardens is a botanical wonderland, with feathery ferns, tall palms and spreading succulents. The sheltered conditions on the island of Tresco, aided by wind- and salt-tolerant Monterey pines and cypresses, have created a sympathetic home for this oasis of some 20,000 plants from 80 countries. These range from spider plants to brilliant flame trees, aromatic myrtle and yellow-flowering acacias. The gardens are scarcely less exuberant in winter when over 60 aloe plants, as well as yuccas from Mexico and Australian banksias, are in full bloom.

Top 10 Features

1. The Plants
2. Valhalla
3. Visitor Centre
4. The Abbey Buildings
5. The Mediterranean Garden
6. The Long Walk
7. The Top Terrace
8. Statuary
9. Magnificent Views
10. Neptune Steps

Exotic plants in bloom

🛈 For a quiet break from the gardens, head down to nearby Appletree Bay, one of the island's best beaches.

🍴 If you don't want to stop in the Gardens' café, try Tresco's New Inn *(see p102)* for tasty bar meals and good beer.

- Map A4
- Tresco, Isles of Scilly, Cornwall
- 01720 424105
- www.tresco.co.uk
- Open 10am–4pm daily
- Adm £12, children under 16 free

◼ The Plants

Visiting Tresco's gardens *(centre)* is like making a horti-cultural world tour. You will see flowered echiums from the Canary Islands, silver trees from South Africa, wine palms from Chile and spiky *agaves* from Mexico.

◼ Valhalla

This exhibition of figure-heads *(above)* and other pieces recovered from ship-wrecks around the islands makes an interesting side-show. The collection, started by Augustus Smith, is named after the mythological Norse palace where the souls of slain heroes feast eternally.

◼ Visitor Centre

Built with trees felled by winter gales, the visitor centre serves teas and lunches, and also has a shop that sells garden guides, seeds and plants.

◼ The Abbey Buildings

The remains of St Nicholas Priory form a harmonious backdrop to the fine foliage. The abbey's archway *(above)* is today an iconic image of Tresco's gardens.

5 The Mediterranean Garden

From the entrance, a startling blue wooden bridge *(above)* leads visitors to the Mediterranean Garden, with a shell house and a fountain at its centre.

6 The Long Walk

Running the length of the gardens, the shaded Long Walk has ferns and Nikau Palms from New Zealand, and large, mature trees such as the Tasmanian Blue Gum with its multiple stems.

7 The Top Terrace

The highest terrace of the gardens is warmer and drier than other parts and hosts plants from Australia and South Africa. Its eastern end overlooks the old Abbey.

8 Statuary

Scattered across the site are exotic statues and sculptures, such as the serenely smiling Earth mother *Gaia* *(above)* next to the Neptune Steps, by sculptor David Wynne.

9 Magnificent Views

Tantalizing glimpses of the ocean *(below)* and neighbouring islands are all around. The best vistas are from Abbey Hill, Olive Terrace in the Mediterranean Garden, and the Top Terrace.

10 Neptune Steps

The granite-carved steps are flanked by clay pots designed by the garden's creator, Augustus Smith, and topped by a giant figure of Neptune, which was once a ship's figurehead.

Emperor of Scilly

Tresco Gardens were founded by Augustus Smith, a key figure in the history of the archipelago, who took over the lease for the islands in 1834. Known as "Emperor Smith of Scilly", he laid the first beds among the abbey ruins after settling on Tresco. Four generations of his family, up to Robert and Lucy Dorrien-Smith who now run the estate, have continued his work.

Porthcurno and the Minack Theatre

One of Cornwall's brightest gems is lovely Porthcurno Bay, cupped between cliffs on the southern coast of the Penwith Peninsula. Though the village itself is low-key, there are enough attractions in the area to merit a visit. The famous open-air Minack Theatre is a unique sight, a magical place to take in some culture and entertainment. Below, the wedge of perfect sandy beach provides plenty of amusement by day, while the coast path to either side runs through a majestic landscape that is managed by the National Trust. Smaller beaches and a scattering of historical relics lie within a short clamber.

Minack Coffee Shop

Visitors with mobility problems can book the viewing platform above the auditorium.

Snacks are available at the Minack Coffee Shop; alternatively try the Porthcurno Beach Café for baguettes and flapjacks (01736 810834).

- Map A6
- Minack Theatre and Exhibition Centre: Porthcurno, Cornwall; 01736 810694
- Exhibition Centre: adm £4.50 adults, child £2.50, senior citizens £3.50
- Minack Box Office: 01736 810181; tickets adm £9–£11.50, under-16 £5–£6 www.minack.com
- Porthcurno Telegraph Museum: Porthcurno, Cornwall; 01736 810966; open Apr–Sep: 10am–5pm daily; adm £6, child £3.40, concession £5.40, students £4.30, family £14.50; www.porthcurno.org.uk

Top 10 Features

1. Logan Rock
2. The View from the Minack
3. The Minack's Rockeries and Gardens
4. Minack Theatre Exhibition Centre
5. Minack Theatre
6. Minack Coffee Shop
7. Porthcurno Telegraph Museum
8. Treryn Dinas Iron Age Fort
9. Pednvounder's White Pyramid
10. Porthcurno Beach

1 Logan Rock

The 70-tonne Logan Rock stands on an outcrop on the eastern edge of Porthcurno Bay *(below)*. It was once said to rock on its perch, but in 1824 a band of sailors dislodged it and now it no longer moves.

2 The View from the Minack

In sunny weather, you could imagine yourself on Italy's precipitous Amalfi coast as you soak in the inspiring view from this cliffside theatre. The jagged headland forms a magnificent backdrop to performances.

3 The Minack's Rockeries and Gardens

The rockeries and gardens surrounding the theatre have become an attraction in their own right. The choice of plants – colourful succulents and hardy shrubs *(below)* – is based on plans by Rowena Cade, the Minack's founder.

4 Minack Theatre Exhibition Centre

This exhibition centre *(above)* tells the remarkable story of the creation of the Minack, which was the inspiration of Rowena Cade in the 1930s.

5 Minack Theatre

On the cliffs above Porthcurno stands Cornwall's most famous theatre – an amphitheatre set into the rock. Over 17 weeks in summer, you can attend a variety of theatrical performances.

6 Minack Coffee Shop

There is no more panoramic spot within miles for a snack than this coffee shop, perched on the cliff edge. It is open only to visitors to the Exhibition Centre and play-goers.

7 Porthcurno Telegraph Museum

In 1870, an undersea cable was laid to North America from Porthcurno. A museum exploring the history of the telegraph system now occupies the terminus, set within a network of tunnels.

8 Treryn Dinas Iron Age Fort

Logan Rock forms part of an Iron Age promontory fort. The few traces that can still be seen include four ramparts, and the remains of stone houses within a ditch across the promontory.

9 Pednvounder's White Pyramid

Halfway along the path to Logan Rock you will come across this peculiar structure *(below)*, placed here in the 1950s to mark the termination of a telegraph cable which once crossed the English Channel to France.

10 Porthcurno Beach

Below the museum, Porthcurno's beach *(above)* is among the finest on the Penwith Peninsula. Sheltered by cliffs on either side, the white sand is mixed with tiny shell fragments. Coastal paths lead to Porth Chapel and Pednvounder beaches.

The Building of the Minack

Rowena Cade purchased the Minack headland for £100. She built a house here and began organizing amateur theatre productions for friends in the 1920s. From this developed the more ambitious idea of an open-air theatre and in 1932 the first production was staged – *The Tempest*. Rowena Cade continued to improve the site until her death in 1983.

TOP 10 St Ives

The port and resort of St Ives is like nowhere else in Britain. Its intricate mesh of lanes – bearing such names as Salubrious Place and Teetotal Street – backs onto a bustling quayside and a quartet of sandy beaches, presenting fetching vistas at every turn. Overlooking one beach is the region's premier art gallery, the Tate St Ives, but there are few streets without a scattering of smaller galleries displaying a range of local landscapes and harbour scenes that recall the town's past and its continuing role as a hive of creativity. Added to these is a dense concentration of restaurants and bars, swish hotels and cosy B&Bs squeezed into tiny, flower-bedecked fishermen's cottages.

A café, Porthmeor Beach

🚗 St Ives is a driver's nightmare. Though often full, the most central car parks are Barnoon, above the Tate, or at the station.

🍴 The Tate's rooftop café is ideal for a snack while you take in the panorama.

• Map B5
• Tourist information: Street an Pol; 09052 522250; www.stivestic.co.uk
• Tate St Ives: Porthmeor Beach; 01736 796226
• St Ives Society of Artists Gallery: Norway Square; 01736 795582
• St Ia: Market Place; 01736 796404
• St Ives Museum, Wheal Dream; 01736 796005
• Leach Pottery: Higher Stennack; 01736 799703
• Barbara Hepworth Museum: Barnoon Hill; 01736 796226; open: Mar–Oct 10am–5:20pm daily; Nov–Feb 10am–4:20pm Tue–Sun

Top 10 Features

1. Tate St Ives
2. St Ives Society of Artists Gallery
3. Porthminster Beach
4. St Ia
5. St Ives Museum
6. St Ives September Festival
7. Trewyn Subtropical Gardens
8. Leach Pottery
9. Porthmeor Beach
10. Barbara Hepworth Museum and Sculpture Garden

1 Tate St Ives
Few British galleries have such a striking setting as this, overlooking a beach. Its circular entrance recalls the gasworks that formerly stood here. The interior is perfect to display local art *(above)*.

2 St Ives Society of Artists Gallery
Housed in the former Mariners Church, this gallery is a good place to take in contemporary work by the Society's members. The Mariners Gallery in the ex-crypt also holds private exhibitions.

3 Porthminster Beach
The largest of St Ives' beaches *(below)* always has space for swimming or lounging and is popular with sand sculptors. The famous Porthminster Beach Café is located here *(see p103)*.

Call the museums and galleries for opening times and admission fees.

St Ives Museum
5
Unearthing this museum in the maze of back streets is like discovering a treasure chest of curiosities. The quirky collection covers every aspect of local history, from geology and archaeology to mining, fishing, farming and shipwrecks.

St Ia
4
This 15th-century parish church *(above)* is dedicated to St Ia, the missionary after whom the town is probably named. It has a wagon roof and a granite font.

St Ives September Festival
6
This boisterous, 15-day festival features comedy, tribute bands, local folk music and African dance. There is also free music spilling from many pubs.

Trewyn Subtropical Gardens
7
In the heart of St Ives, this quiet retreat *(above)* with banana trees and other subtropical plants is a peaceful spot even in high season, and makes for an ideal picnic venue.

Leach Pottery
8
Britain's foremost potter, Bernard Leach (1887–1979), established this pottery in 1920 to create his Japanese-inspired work *(right)*. Today, you can see exhibitions of his work and watch contemporary ceramicists at work.

Porthmeor Beach
9
Backed by cafés and the façade of the Tate gallery, and with the promontory of the island at its eastern end, Porthmeor *(centre)* is the most accessible beach in St Ives. Its firm sand is ideal for castle-building and beach gear can be rented.

Barbara Hepworth Museum and Sculpture Garden
10
Sculptor Barbara Hepworth was at the core of the mid-20th-century arts scene in St Ives. Her studio is now one of Cornwall's most compelling galleries, displaying her mainly abstract works. Larger pieces are arranged around the lush garden (see p97).

Art in St Ives

Sometime in 1920, potters Bernard Leach and Shoji Hamada settled in St Ives to set up Leach Pottery. A stream of artists followed, including sculptor Barbara Hepworth and painter Ben Nicholson in 1939. Along with later arrivals such as Patrick Heron and Terry Frost, they specialized in abstract works strongly influenced by the Cornish landscape.

An Art Pass gives unlimited access for seven days to Tate St Ives, Barbara Hepworth Museum and Sculpture Garden and Leach Pottery.

🔟 Penzance and St Michael's Mount

The port of Penzance sits in the northern end of Mount's Bay. Georgian buildings characterize much of the town, though its harbourside pool is strictly Art Deco. The town has two excellent galleries that continue in the tradition of the colony of artists who settled in neighbouring Newlyn. Across Mount's Bay, St Michael's Mount (centre) makes an eye-catching sight. Originally a priory dedicated to the Archangel St Michael and marking the southern end of a pilgrim's route, St Michael's Way, the structure was later fortified. Visitors who brave the steep climb to the house are rewarded by stunning views.

Market Jew Street
Penzance's main street *(above)* derives its name from the Cornish "Marghas Yow", which means Thursday Market. The domed Market House is at its very top.

The Admiral Benbow Inn

⑨ The terraced and walled gardens are worth a wander and offer excellent views.

- Map B5
- Tourist office: Station Approach, Penzance; 01736 335530; www.westcornwall.org.uk
- Morrab Gardens: Penzance; 01736 336605; adm free; open daily; www.morrabgardens.co.uk • The Exchange: Princes St, Penzance; 01736 363715; adm free
- Newlyn Art Gallery: New Rd, Newlyn; 01736 363715; adm free; www.newlynartgallery.co.uk • Penlee House: Morrab Rd, Penzance; 01736 363625; adm £4.50, free Sat; www.penleehouse.org.uk
- St Michael's Mount: Marazion; 01736 710507; castle: adm £8, family £20; garden: adm £5; child £2, ferry £2 each way, child £1; www.stmichaelsmount.co.uk

Top 10 Features

1. Market Jew Street
2. Chapel Street
3. Morrab Gardens
4. The Exchange
5. Newlyn
6. Penlee House
7. The Causeway, St Michael's Mount
8. The Blue Drawing Room, St Michael's Mount
9. The Chapel, St Michael's Mount
10. The Chevy Chase Room, St Michael's Mount

Chapel Street
Handsome Chapel Street has some of Penzance's comeliest buildings, including the flamboyant Egyptian House *(above)*, dating from 1830. Across the road is the Union Hotel which features a minstrels' gallery.

Morrab Gardens
Just off the town centre, these gardens, built in the 1840s, feature sub-tropical plants, including agaves and bamboos, set around a Victorian bandstand and fountain.

The Exchange
Behind an impressive glass façade, the ground floor of the town's old telephone exchange boasts the largest single exhibition space within 300 km (180 miles).

Call the sights to check opening times.

St Michael's Mount

Newlyn

To the south of Penzance and within a walkable distance, Newlyn is a busy fishing port *(above)* with a thriving early-morning fish market. Attractions include the Newlyn Art Gallery, which showcases contemporary art.

Penlee House

The Newlyn school of artists who settled in the area in the late 19th century *(see p35)* are well-represented in this Victorian gallery and museum set within a park *(right)*. The exhibits reflect the town's fishing and mining heritage.

The Causeway, St Michael's Mount

Off the Marazion coast, the promontory on which St Michael's Mount stands can be reached by boat, but at low tide, you can walk across on a causeway.

The Blue Drawing Room, St Michael's Mount

This exquisite room in a Rococo style has furnishings in a delightful Wedgwood Blue.

The Chapel, St Michael's Mount

A door from the Blue Drawing Room leads into the Priory Church, at the summit of the island. The church is still regularly used for services. The walls are lined with memorials to the St Aubyn family, who have held the castle since 1659.

The Chevy Chase Room, St Michael's Mount

This room is named after its 17th-century plaster frieze depicting hunting scenes described in the *Ballad of Chevy Chase*. A Jacobean oak table *(left)* dominates the room.

St Michael's Mount – History and Legend

Built as a Benedictine priory in 1135 by the Abbot of Mont St Michel in Normandy, France, St Michael's Mount was granted to Colonel John St Aubyn after the Civil War. His descendants have held it ever since. However, legend has it that the mount was the lair of Comoran the giant, who came ashore to steal sheep and was killed by a boy, Jack.

Visiting St Michael's Mount is unsuitable for people with mobility problems.

29

🔟 Padstow

Tucked into the Camel Estuary, Padstow is one of Cornwall's most attractive ports. Lively and smart, the town is well-placed for beaches, with some of the county's best – Daymer, Polzeath, Trevone, Constantine – within a short distance. This is mainly a fishing port whose catch is taken daily to auctions at Brixham and Newlyn, though plenty also ends up in local eateries. Foodies will know the town primarily as the domain of celebrity seafood chef Rick Stein, who has raised Padstow's profile with his luxury hotels and seafood restaurants, which are among the best in the country. Such is his grip on the place that it has been nicknamed "Padstein".

Rick Stein's Café

🕑 **Enquire at the tourist office about open-air brass band concerts, performed on most Sundays and some weekdays in summer.**

- Map D3
- Tourist information: North Quay; 01841 533449
- Rick Stein's restaurants: see p87 (St Petroc's Bistro; The Seafood Restaurant; Stein's Fish & Chips)
- Prideaux Place: 01841 532411; open Apr–Sep: 1:30–5pm Sun–Thu, last tour 4pm; adm £8.50; grounds £3; www.prideauxplace.co.uk
- Padstow Museum: Market Place; 01841 532752; open Apr–Oct: 10:30am–4:30pm Mon–Fri, 10:30am–1pm Sat
- St Petroc's Church: Church St; 01841 533776
- National Lobster Hatchery: South Quay; 01841 533877; open 10am daily, closing times vary; adm £3.75

Top 10 Features

1. Padstow Harbour
2. The Camel Trail
3. Rick Stein's Restaurants
4. The Camel Estuary
5. Prideaux Place
6. Padstow Museum
7. Obby Oss
8. The Saints' Way
9. St Petroc's Church
10. The National Lobster Hatchery

Padstow Harbour
The town's inner harbour *(right)* is where crowds gather to see the catch being brought in. On the quayside is Abbey House, Padstow's oldest building. Explore the estuary on boat trips.

The Camel Trail
This is Cornwall's finest walking and cycling route *(below)*. It follows the track of a disused railway line alongside the River Camel for 34 km (17 miles). You can rent bikes from Padstow and Wadebridge.

Rick Stein's Restaurants
Sample delightful seafood at The Seafood Restaurant. The culinary master also runs five hotels, a café, a deli, a patisserie and a fish and chips takeaway in Padstow.

The Camel Estuary
The major river on Cornwall's northern coast, the Camel is a haven for wading migrant birds that feed on the fertile mudflats. It derives its name from the Cornish *cam pol*, or winding river. Passenger ferries cross the estuary from Padstow to Rock.

You can find more information at www.padstowlive.com.

Prideaux Place

On a hill overlooking the town, this Elizabethan manor house *(above)* has richly furnished rooms and superlative plasterwork. Outside are formal gardens and a deer park. The films *Twelfth Night* and *Oscar and Lucinda* were shot here.

Padstow Museum

Housed in the Old Institute building, this little museum is crowded with archaeological items, nautical models, old photos and a scary Obby Oss costume.

Obby Oss

One of Cornwall's most flamboyant festivals *(above)* takes place on May 1 or 2. Processions around the town are led by a figure in an outlandish costume *(see p39)*.

The Saints' Way

Crossing the peninsula between Padstow and Fowey, this 45-km (28-mile) trail traces the route taken by pilgrims. It follows ancient footpaths and quiet country lanes. The official starting point in Padstow is St Petroc's Church.

St Petroc's Church

Padstow was once known as Petrocstowe, from the missionary St Petroc, who is said to have crossed the Irish Sea on a cabbage leaf. The church is famous for the Prideaux-Brune memorial *(above)* and the 15th- or 16th-century font carved from Catacleuse stone.

The National Lobster Hatchery

Get up close to various crustaceans at this fascinating exhibition. The tanks hold creatures such as spider crabs, crayfish and sponges, varying in size from inch-long baby lobsters to the residential giants.

The Obby Oss Tale

The origins of Obby Oss are lost but it includes elements of many other May Day festivities, and is similar to one held in Minehead, Somerset. Controlled by club-wielding "Teazers", the Obby Oss figures, in twirling hooped gowns, are probably intended to drive winter away, while spring is represented by the white-clothed escort. The festivities begin the previous night when the Blue Ribbon Oss emerges from the Golden Lion pub.

Left **Buckfast Abbey** Right **Reconstructed Anglo-Saxon village**

🔟 Moments in History

1 50–55 AD: Roman Invasion

The Romans occupied Exeter and established a strong garrison there without penetrating further west, where Celtic tribes held sway. The region benefited from the Roman occupation, though few vestiges of that culture remain.

2 6th and 7th Centuries: Anglo-Saxon Settlements

During Roman withdrawal, Saxon tribes began to settle in the region, but made little headway against the Celtic tribes, whose strongholds were concentrated in Cornwall. The Arthurian legends are probably derived from the exploits of one of the Celtic chieftains, who continued to resist the Anglo-Saxons.

3 11th to 16th Centuries: The Wool Industry

Devon's wool industry flourished under the stability imposed by the Normans. Land-owners of fertile inland pastures built mansions and merchants exported produce to Europe from the southern ports, which grew rich.

4 1530s: Dissolution of the Monasteries

The great monastic houses, which wielded huge influence and power in Devon and Cornwall, were suppressed by order of Henry VIII. Some, like the Benedictine abbey of Tavistock, were destroyed; others, like Buckfast Abbey, became mansions of wealthy merchants.

5 1558–1603: The Elizabethan Era

Devon became a strategic region during the contest against Spain. Exeter and Plymouth in particular were important military and naval bases. The great western sea-ports benefited from the expansion of transatlantic trade and the first English colonists of the New World set sail from here.

6 1642–51: The Civil War

Most of the region sided with the Royalists during England's Civil War, though both Exeter and Plymouth originally supported the Roundheads (Parliamentarians). Charles I defeated the Earl of Essex's army in 1644 but Royalists were checked by Thomas Fairfax's army. This led to the fall of Pendennis Castle and Exeter in 1646.

7 18th Century: Tin and Copper Mining

Under the Normans, Cornwall had become Europe's biggest source of tin. A series

Statue of John Wesley

Preceding pages **Boats moored at St Ives harbour**

Remains of Wheal Basset tin mine

of scientific advances in the 18th century allowed the tin and copper mining industry to become highly profitable. Copper mining, concentrated around Redruth and Camborne, peaked in the 1840s.

1743–86: Spread of Wesleyism

The impoverished conditions of the region's miners led to widespread acceptance of the Methodist preaching of John Wesley. Methodist chapels are still standing in the region today.

1884 onwards: Artists' Colonies Established

Drawn by intense light, dramatic seascapes and the life of fishing communities, painter Stanhope Forbes settled in Newlyn in 1884 and became the leading figure in the artists' colony. Neighbouring St Ives continues to be an important artistic hub.

1939–45: World War II

Although most of the West Country was designated safe from German attack and received evacuees from London and the Midlands, Plymouth suffered the worst bombing of any British seaport. Exeter was also targeted in the "Baedeker raids", which were aimed at cultural centres mentioned in Baedeker guidebooks.

Top 10 Arthurian Sites

1 Tintagel Castle
The most evocative of all Arthurian sights is believed to be his birthplace *(see p83)*.

2 Slaughterbridge
This spot on Bodmin Moor is said to be the site of King Arthur's last battle, against his nephew Mordred. Ⓢ *Map E3*

3 Dozmary Pool
It is said that Arthur's sword, Excalibur, was thrown here and received by the Lady of the Lake. Ⓢ *Map E3*

4 The Tristan Stone
This monument marks the grave of Drustanus, identified with Tristan (or Tristram), one of Arthur's knights. Ⓢ *Map E4*

5 Lyonnesse
A fabled land sunk beneath the waves, Lyonnesse is a candidate for Arthur's birthplace. Ⓢ *Map A6*

6 Loe Pool
Like Dozmary Pool, this is where Excalibur was believed to be restored to the Lady of the Lake. Ⓢ *Map B6*

7 Camelford
This town on Bodmin Moor is one of several places identified with Camelot. Ⓢ *Map E3*

8 Castle Dore
An Iron Age hillfort said to have been King Mark of Cornwall's home *(see p94)*.

9 Boscastle
After his last battle, Arthur's body was supposedly transported to this North Cornwall fishing port. Ⓢ *Map D2*

10 Castle an Dinas
This important hillfort outside St Columb Major is believed to be Arthur's hunting lodge. Ⓢ *Map D4*

Left **A woodland path on the Saints' Way** Right **St Michael's Way**

🔟 Great Walks

1 Hall Walk

One of the best short walks in Cornwall, this 6-km (4-mile) amble explores the area around Fowey. Passing through woods overlooking the harbour and river, the path climbs above Pont Pill – where you may spot herons and curlews – and takes in a memorable panorama from Penleath Point. ◈ *Map E4*

2 Two Moors Way/Coast to Coast Walk

The Two Moors Way, which links Exmoor and Dartmoor, can be extended at its southern end between Ivybridge and Plymouth to make a 180-km (112-mile) coast-to-coast hike. The most dramatic scenery is on Dartmoor, though Lynmouth at the northern end makes a striking starting point or finishing post. ◈ *Map J1–K1*

3 Hobby Drive

Above the chocolate-box village of Clovelly, this shady 5-km (3-mile) stroll affords glorious views over the harbour and Bideford Bay. Spring is the best time, when beech leaves shimmer above carpets of bluebells. ◈ *Map G2*

4 Saints' Way

Cornwall's coast-to-coast trail covers about 48 km (30 miles) between Padstow and Fowey. Though there is no evidence of the whole route being used in the Middle Ages, parts of it were certainly travelled by pilgrims en route to shrines, holy wells and chapels. ◈ *Map D3*

5 Tarka Trail

Inspired by Henry Williamson's animal tale *Tarka the Otter (see p68)*, this figure-of-eight route centring on Barnstaple takes in coastal and inland areas of North Devon. If you include the section covered by the Tarka Line between Eggesford and Barnstaple, the route is 288 km (180 miles) long *(see p67)*.

Crossing moorland on the Two Moors Way

The Tarka Trail and Dartmoor Way are suitable for cyclists, while the South West Coast Path has stretches suitable for wheelchairs.

Dart Valley Trail

6 You can experience the glories of the Dart Valley on this 26-km (16-mile) walk, which swoops high above or runs alongside the River Dart. Half of it is a circuit, involving two ferry crossings, and the other half follows the river to Totnes. ◈ Map J5

Dartmoor Way

7 This circular route of 153 km (95 miles) crosses some of Dartmoor's most thrilling terrain, including rugged moor, wooded valleys and disused railway tracks. Much of the trail – like the area between Tavistock and Okehampton – skirts the edge of the moor, but it also takes in Princetown in the centre of Dartmoor. ◈ Map J4

South West Coast Path

8 England's longest National Trail – 1,014 km (630 miles) – is used by anyone who walks for any length along the Devon and Cornwall seaboard. Kicking off in Minehead in Somerset, winding along the indented coasts of Devon, Cornwall and finally Dorset, the trail is predominantly hilly and often scenically dramatic.

East Devon Way

9 Also known as the Foxglove Way, this undulating inland trail follows footpaths, bridleways and lanes between Exmouth and Uplyme, north of Lyme Regis over the Dorset border. It is 61 km (38 miles) long. ◈ Map L4

St Michael's Way

10 Weaving a meandering route between Lelant, near St Ives, and Marazion, this 19.5-km (12.5-mile) trail was once used by pilgrims and travellers to avoid the treacherous waters around Land's End. ◈ Map B5

Top 10 Outdoor Activities

1 **Horse-Riding**
Stables exist all over the region and offer escorted treks for riders of all abilities.

2 **Hiking**
The simplest (and cheapest) way to experience the beauty of the region.

3 **Canoeing**
The rivers of Dartmoor and the great waterways of Cornwall can be enjoyed on a canoe trip.

4 **Coasteering**
This increasingly popular pursuit involves negotiating rocky coasts using a variety of means.

5 **Sailing**
Salcombe, Dartmouth, Falmouth and Fowey offer facilities for sailors of all levels.

6 **Surfing**
Some of Britain's top surfing beaches can be found in the West Country, with annual competitions at Newquay.

7 **Windsurfing**
The region's bays and inlets are ideal for windsurfers, with rental equipment available at many places.

8 **Diving**
The wrecks and reefs of Devon and Cornwall draw diving enthusiasts from far and wide.

9 **Gig Racing**
Ex-pilot boats are raced off the coastal villages of West Cornwall in summer, most famously in the Isles of Scilly.

10 **Sea Safaris**
Take to the seas on organized whale-, seal- and shark-watching excursions during summer.

Left **Morris dancers at Sidmouth Folk Week** Right **Tar barrelling**

Festivals

Helston's Flora Day
This Cornish extravaganza is truly unique, involving a stately procession of top-hatted people in frocks performing the "Furry Dance" through the streets of Helston. Flowers and sprigs of sycamore are a feature of this spring festival. *Map B5 • May 8 (or previous Sat if date falls on Sun or Mon)*

St Ives September Festival
The arts have long had a strong presence in St Ives and this two-week jamboree brings them together with exhibitions, drama and poetry readings. Music ranges from cello recitals to tribute pop acts and African beats, with most performances held in St Ia church and the Guildhall. There are also talks and comedy acts. *Map B5 • Mid-Sep • www.stivesseptemberfestival.co.uk*

Fowey Festival of Words and Music
Run by the Daphne du Maurier Society, this 10-day literary festival celebrates the author, who lived in Fowey, and features music, drama, walks, workshops and daily talks by well-known personalities. *Map E4 • Mid-May • www.foweyfestival.com*

Sidmouth Folk Week
Folk music, Northumbrian pipes and Morris dancers feature at a seaside festival in one of Devon's most elegant towns. Even non-folk fans succumb to the event's upbeat charm, with buskers lining the Esplanade and pubs jammed with carousers. Accommodation and concert tickets sell out quickly. *Map L4 • Early Aug • www.sidmouthfolkweek.co.uk*

Tar Barrelling, Ottery St Mary
Every Bonfire Night barrels that have been soaked in tar are set alight and hoisted around town. Each of Ottery's central pubs sponsors a barrel – 17 in all. The evening culminates in fireworks around a huge bonfire beside the River Otter. *Map L3 • Nov 5 (or previous Sat if date falls on Sun or Mon)*

Padstow's Obby Oss character

Golowan Festival, Penzance

This week-long arts and dance festival features processions, circus performers, buskers and a mock mayoral election. The Golowan Band provides music, while flaming torches and fire-works add to the spectacle. ⊗ *Map B5 • Late Jun • www.golowan.org*

Dartmouth Royal Regatta

The three-day regatta highlights the town's nautical traditions with rowing races and yachting displays. It became "royal" after an unscheduled visit by Queen Victoria in 1856. The festival has a distinct martial flavour with military bands and an exciting air display by the RAF *(see p80)*.

Obby Oss, Padstow

Pagan fertility rites and local traditions unite in this May Day spectacle. The main character, the Obby Oss, garbed in a black costume draped around a 2-m (6-ft) wide hoop, is accompanied by a "Teazer" with music, drums and the May Song. ⊗ *Map D3 • May 1 (or May 2 if date falls on Sun)*

Oyster Festival, Falmouth

This four-day event pays homage to Cornish seafood. There's music from the local brass band, oyster-shucking competitions, cookery demonstrations and boat races. ⊗ *Map C5 • Mid-Oct • www.falmouthoysterfestival.co.uk*

Lowender Peran, Perranporth

Cornwall's Celtic heritage is the theme of this festival, which features music, poetry and acts from Scottish, Irish, Welsh, Manx and Breton performers. ⊗ *Map C4 • Mid-Oct • www.lowenderperan.co.uk*

Top 10 Live Music and Theatre Venues

1 Exeter Phoenix
Exeter's premier arts centre. ⊗ *Map P2 • Gandy St • 01392 66 7080 • www.exeterphoenix.org.uk*

2 Eden Project
This is Cornwall's best outdoor music venue in summer *(see pp10–11)*.

3 The Cavern, Exeter
Bands play nightly at this underground venue. ⊗ *Map P2 • 83–4 Queen St • 01392 495370 • www.exetercavern.com*

4 Hall for Cornwall, Truro
Drama and music are staged here. ⊗ *Map C5 • Back Quay, Truro • 01872 262466 • www.hallforcornwall.co.uk*

5 Exeter Northcott
Exeter's principal theatre venue. ⊗ *Map N1 • Stocker Rd • 01392 493493 • www.exeternorthcott.co.uk*

6 Minack Theatre
This cliff-top amphitheatre hosts a range of productions in summer *(see pp24–5)*.

7 Acorn Arts Centre
This former church is now a playhouse. ⊗ *Map B5 • Parade St, Penzance • 01736 363545 • www.theacornpenzance.com*

8 Plymouth Pavilions
A large, multi-purpose complex. ⊗ *Map N5 • Millbay Rd, Plymouth • 08451 461460 • www.plymouthpavilions.com*

9 Barbican Theatre
Theatre specializing in new drama. ⊗ *Map Q6 • Castle St, Plymouth • 01752 267131 • www.barbicantheatre.co.uk*

10 Theatre Royal
Mainstream shows are held in the main venue; cutting-edge work in the Drum Theatre. ⊗ *Map P5 • Royal Parade, Plymouth • 01752 267222 • www.theatreroyal.com*

Left **Porthcurno Beach** Right **Whitesand Bay**

Great Beaches

1 Porthcurno

One of the finest bays of the Penwith Peninsula, Porthcurno, with its wedge of white sand mixed with tiny shells, is squeezed between granite cliffs. The rock-hewn Minack Theatre is located to one side and there is a museum of telegraphy at the back of the beach. Pubs and cafés can be found close by (see pp24–5).

2 Par Beach, Isles of Scilly

Majestic, bare and wild, the beaches on St Martin's are considered to be the best on the Isles of Scilly. Par Beach on the island's southern shore is probably the most impressive – a long, empty strand looking out onto rocks that make up the Eastern Isles. Be prepared for chilly water though. ◈ Map B4

3 Whitesand Bay

This expanse of fine sand close to Land's End is a favourite with surfers and families alike.

It has a good beachside café and at Sennen Cove, the more popular southern end of the beach, is the Old Success Inn. Surfing equipment is available for hire and courses are also provided. ◈ Map A5

4 Kynance Cove

This is one of the best options on the Lizard Peninsula, where beaches are few and far between. The 10-minute walk from the car park is well worth the trudge for the beach's fine white sands, rocky spires and surrounding grassy areas. Swimming is limited by the tides but other attractions include caves and cliffs with serpentine seams of sand. ◈ Map B6

5 Woolacombe Bay

Surf dudes come from far and wide to one of the West Country's most famous surfing beaches. The beach is popular with families and there is a warren of dunes behind for

The rocky shore at Kynance Cove

A list of accessible beaches is available at www.accessiblecountryside.org.uk.

The beach at Fistral Bay

exploring. Crowds gather at the northern end, but more space can be found at the quieter southern end. The small resort of Woolacombe has shops and cafés (see p67).

Fistral Bay
Surf aficionados flock to this beach, which is the venue for surfing competitions. A surf centre supplies equipment for hire. Most of the sand is covered by water at high tide and strong currents mean that kids need to be careful, though lifeguards are present throughout the summer. The restaurants and cafés here offer outdoor seating. ◈ Map C4

Watergate Bay
North of Newquay, this arc of golden sand has a wild appeal. It is home to the Extreme Academy, which offers kite-surfing, land-boarding and other pursuits for the adventurous. Behind it are Jamie Oliver's famous restaurant Fifteen, and the more casual Beach Hut (see p87), both with splendid views. Watergate is not very sheltered, so make sure you carry wind-breakers. ◈ Map C4

Tunnels Beach, Ilfracombe
This private beach is named after the tunnels that have provided access to it since 1823, when the swimming was segregated. There is a tidal bathing pool and on-duty lifeguards make the beach safe for kids. The rock pooling is top-class and there are kayaks for hire. ◈ Map H1 • Bath Place, Ilfracombe • 01271 879882 • Open Apr–Sep: 10am–6pm daily; Jul–Aug: 10am–7pm; Oct: 10am–5pm Tue–Sun • Adm • www.tunnelsbeaches.co.uk

Croyde Bay
Sandwiched between the extensive west-facing Saunton Sands and Woolacombe, this compact bay has fine sand. There are campsites around and the village has pubs and bars that fill up in the evenings. ◈ Map H1

Blackpool Sands
Backed by woods and meadows, this family-friendly beach makes an enticing sight as it swings into view on the road from Dartmouth. Its sheltered location, clear water and fine sand make it one of South Devon's best swimming spots. For refreshments there is the renowned Venus Café. ◈ Map K6

Left **Scones with jam and cream** Right **Rick Stein's Café, popular for fish and chips**

Culinary Specialities

Yarg Cheese
This moist cheese from Bodmin Moor has a covering of nettles and is the best known of a crop of Cornish cheeses to have appeared in recent years. There is also a version with a garlic flavour.

Star Gazy Pie
According to legend, this pie originated when Tom Bawcock, a fisherman from the Cornish village of Mousehole, braved fierce storms to provide fish for the starving villagers. Eaten on Tom Bawcock's Eve (December 23), the pie contains pilchards and five other kinds of fish, their heads poking through the crust, as if gazing skyward.

Devonshire pasties

Beer
Though Devon and Cornwall have traditionally been known for their cider consumption, local breweries have achieved fame for their real ale. St Austell is the biggest regional outfit, responsible for Tribute ale, which is exported nationwide. There are several excellent microbrews as well, including Spingo, which is made and drunk only in Helston *(see p59)*.

Pilchards
Once the mainstay of the fishing industry in the West, pilchards had almost disappeared from local waters by 1914 due to being overfished. Since then, numbers have recovered but the catch is mostly exported. They can still be sampled in some restaurants, however, and are best eaten between July and November.

Cream Teas
The traditional cream tea consists of scones fresh from the oven, thickly churned clotted cream and lashings of strawberry jam. According to some, in

The tea room at Dwelling House

Devon the cream is placed onto the half-scone first, then the jam; in Cornwall the jam is spread first and topped with cream.

Lobster
Lobster pots piled high in fishing ports attest to the abundance of lobster off the coasts of Devon and Cornwall. This delicacy can be barbecued or grilled, but usually tastes best simply boiled.

Pasties
Originally made for miners in Cornwall, this crimped pastry case with a meat and vegetable filling is ubiquitous in Devon too. The usual filling is beef, swede and potato, but it can also be anything else. According to tradition, the top crimp is said to be Devonian in style, while the side crimp is authentically Cornish.

Wine
Sharpham in Devon and Camel Valley in Cornwall are two of Britain's most renowned wineries. Camel Valley also produces its own champagne-type fizz, "Cornwall".

Fish and Chips
The ports and resorts of Devon and Cornwall are among the best places to sample fish and chips. Superior outlets include Rick Stein's in Padstow (see pp30 and 87).

Crab
Some of the country's best crab comes from ports in Devon and Cornwall, such as Brixham and Port Isaac. Spider, blue velvet and brown crabs are the best varieties, and form the basis of a great salad or sandwich filling. Avoid eating them from January to March.

Top 10 Places for Cream Teas

1 Otterton Mill
Fine organic scones are made in this ancient mill.
◎ Map L4 • Otterton, Budleigh Salterton • 01395 567041

2 Falmouth Hotel
Nibble scones on the terrace of this Victorian hotel.
◎ Map C5 • Castle Beach, Falmouth • 01326 312671

3 New Yard, Trelowarren
Cream teas are served in this estate's stableyard.
◎ Map B5 • Mawgan, Helston • 01326 221595

4 Dwelling House
Scones and an excellent choice of cakes in a cosy, eclectic tea room (see p95).

5 Primrose Cottage
Possibly Devon's best teas and cakes. ◎ Map K5 • Lustleigh, Newton Abbot • 01647 277365

6 Southern Cross
A walled garden provides the perfect setting for tea.
◎ Map L4 • Newton Poppleford, nr Sidmouth • 01395 568439

7 Georgian Tea Room
Choose from the selection of home-made cakes. ◎ Map K4 • Broadway House, 35 High St, Topsham • 01392 873465

8 Watersmeet House
Beautiful spot by the river for tea and cakes (see p71).

9 Combe House
Delicate sandwiches, shortbread, fruit tartlets and champagne are served in a luxurious setting (see p114).

10 Rectory Farm and Tea Rooms
Feast in a 13th-century farmhouse beside an open fire. ◎ Map E2 • Crosstown, Morwenstow, near Bude • 01288 331251

For restaurants in Devon and Cornwall See pp71, 81, 87, 95 and 103.

Left **Tintagel Castle** Right **St Mawes Castle**

TOP 10 Castles

1 Caerhays Castle
John Nash – architect of Buckingham Palace – designed this fantasy-Gothic structure in 1810, and it is now a private home. The real showpiece is the garden, with its magnolias and rhododendrons. The adjacent curve of beach is also an excellent destination *(see p94)*.

2 Powderham Castle
This seat of the earls of Devon has been built in a mix of architectural styles. The dominant flavour is 18th century, as seen in the ornate Music Room, designed by renowned architect James Wyatt, and the lavish Rococo Staircase Hall *(see p75)*.

3 Pendennis Castle
The most westerly of the artillery forts built under Henry VIII, Pendennis and its twin St Mawes were built to safeguard the port of Falmouth, the "key to Cornwall". The castle's ramparts and bastions were erected in around 1600 and the gun batteries were added during the Napoleonic wars *(see p97)*.

Caerhays Castle

Powderham Castle

4 Berry Pomeroy Castle
This romantic ruin on the edge of a wooded ravine is reputed to be haunted. Built by the Pomeroy family in the 15th century, the castle was abandoned 200 years later. Ever since, there have been reported sightings of the ghosts of the "White Lady" and the "Blue Lady". ⊗ *Map K5 • Totnes • 01803 866618 • Open Apr–Sep: 10am–6pm daily; Oct: 10am–4pm daily; Nov–Mar: 10am–4pm Sat & Sun • Adm • www.english-heritage.org.uk*

5 St Mawes Castle
The most elaborately decorated of Henry VIII's coastal fortresses, this castle follows a clover-leaf design, with round walls that were intended to deflect enemy fire. However, the castle was never tested in war – it surrendered without putting up a fight to Parliamentarian forces in 1646 *(see p34)*. Visitors can tour the gun rooms, governor's quarters, barracks and kitchen *(see p92)*.

Castle Drogo

This 20th-century fortress in the Teign Valley was designed to resemble a medieval stronghold by architect Edwin Lutyens, who was instructed by retail tycoon Julius Drewe to create a replica of the castles of yore. Austere granite walls and a warren of stone corridors give the castle a spartan feel. You can play croquet here in summer *(see p12)*.

Okehampton Castle

This Norman castle on a spur above the River Okement is a dramatic sight, dominated by the remains of its keep. The fortress, once owned by the Courtenay family – later earls of Devon – was mainly used as a hunting lodge. Picnics can be enjoyed at the old deer park *(see p12)*.

Compton Castle

This buttressed manor house has been home to the seafaring Gilbert family – related to Sir Walter Raleigh – for nearly 600 years. Film-makers have long been attracted to its theatrical façade – Ang Lee filmed *Sense and Sensibility* here in 1995.
🏵 *Map K5 • Marldon, Paignton*
• 01803 661906 • Open Apr–Oct:
10:30am–4:30pm Tue–Thu • Adm
• www.nationaltrust.org.uk

Okehampton Castle

Tintagel Castle

Set on a promontory above the turbulent Atlantic, the forlorn ruins of Tintagel resemble a fairy-tale castle. Said to be the birthplace of the mythical King Arthur, the castle was in fact a Norman stronghold *(see p83)*.

Totnes Castle

Towering above the centre of Totnes, this classic Norman construction was erected after the Conquest *(see p34)* to overawe the Saxon town. The stone keep was added later. 🏵 *Map K5*
• Totnes • 01803 864406 • Open Apr–Sep: 10am–6pm daily; Oct: 10am–5pm daily; Nov: 10am–4pm Sat & Sun
• Adm • www.english-heritage.org.uk

Left **Exeter Cathedral** Centre **Truro Cathedral** Right **St Neot's church**

🔟 Churches, Abbeys and Cathedrals

St Nonna

Known as the "cathedral of the moors", this 15th-century church on Bodmin Moor is famous for its 79 bench-ends carved with saints, clowns and musicians. The Norman font with its fierce faces has been imitated in local churches. The "vicar of Altarnun" features in Daphne du Maurier's novel *Jamaica Inn*.
◈ *Map E3 • Altarnun*
• *Open 10am–4pm daily*

Truro Cathedral

Rising tall over Truro, this Neo-Gothic monument was the first Anglican cathedral to be constructed in England since St Paul's in London. Built between 1880 and 1910, it incorporates the old parish church of St Mary's, which has occupied the spot for 600 years. Highlights include Jacobean tombs and Victorian stained glass *(see p92)*.

Exeter Cathedral

Surrounded by the grassy Cathedral Close and crowned by twin Norman towers, Exeter Cathedral is the grandest of Devon and Cornwall's churches. The 15th-century Exeter Clock and Chapter House, the 14th-century Minstrels' Gallery and carvings on the choir stalls are among the main attractions *(see pp20–21)*.

Buckfast Abbey

Buckfast Abbey

This complex on the banks of the River Dart was founded in the 11th century, rebuilt as a Cistercian abbey in 1147, dissolved in 1539 and rebuilt by Benedictine monks between 1907 and 1937. Today, visitors can admire the striking stained-glass windows of the abbey and purchase home-made specialities made by the monks, such as tonic wine and beeswax *(see p80)*.

St Neot

Located in one of Bodmin Moor's prettiest villages, this 15th-century church contains stained-glass windows depicting Noah's Ark and St Neot himself. The churchyard boasts what is claimed to be Cornwall's finest ornamental cross. ◈ *Map E3*
• *St Neot, Cornwall • 01579 320472*

St Nonna's church

6 Church of the Holy Cross

The grandeur of this red sandstone structure reflects the former importance of Crediton, which grew wealthy on wool but is now just a village. The church is perpendicular in style, with generous windows illuminating its rich interior. The east window celebrates Crediton's most famous son, St Boniface.

7 St Mary

Set on a hill in poet Samuel Taylor Coleridge's native town, stately St Mary dates from the 13th century. It was enlarged a century later by John de Grandisson, Bishop of Exeter. Noteworthy features include a still working 14th-century astronomical clock and the Apostles Window, the church's exquisite west window. ✆ Map L3 • College Rd, Ottery St Mary • 01404 812062 • www.otterystmary.org.uk

8 St Just-in-Roseland

Situated on the Roseland peninsula, this church on the shore of a creek is surrounded by palms and magnolias. The church dates from 1261, but its battlement tower was added in the 15th century. ✆ Map C5 • St Just-in-Roseland • 01326 270248 • www.stjust.roselandchurches.co.uk

The façade of St Mary

9 St Enodoc

This tiny 13th-century church is located in the middle of a golf course within sight of the Camel Estuary. The churchyard holds the grave of the poet John Betjeman who lived for a time in nearby Trebetherick (see p86).

10 St Petroc's Church

Built around 1470, the largest parish church in Cornwall has a typical Cornish wagon roof. Look out for the superb Norman font that showcases angels, demons and interlacing trees of life. ✆ Map D4 • Bodmin • 01208 737867 • www.st-petroc-bodmin.co.uk

Left **Trengwainton Gardens** Right **Bicton Park**

TOP 10 Great Gardens

1 Lost Gardens of Heligan

There is an air of mystery about this "lost garden". First planted in the late 18th century, the garden was neglected to the point of decay until it was rediscovered by Tim Smit, the guiding light behind the Eden Project *(see pp10–11)*. Smit restored the garden's main features while preserving its wild, tangled character. The site includes an Italian Garden, walled flower gardens and a subtropical "Jungle" valley *(see p91)*.

2 Trelissick Garden

Sheltered by woodlands, this Cornish garden features the national collection of photinias and azaras. Bordering the River Fal, the site affords views across the Carrick Roads Estuary *(see p93)*.

3 Trengwainton Gardens

Visitors to this diverse garden can enjoy an abundance of exotic trees, shrubs, sheltered walled gardens and a woodland area. In spring, the blooming azaleas, camellias and rhododendrons add to the colourful display. Plan a picnic by the stream or cherish the view of the Lizard Peninsula from the terrace. ✆ *Map B5 • Madron, Penzance • 01736 363148 • Open mid-Feb–Oct: 10:30am–5pm Sun–Thu • Adm • www.nationaltrust.org.uk*

4 Trebah

The subtropical garden has water gardens with Koi carp and glades of 100-year-old tree ferns. Plants have been introduced from around the world, including Gunnera (giant rhubarb) from Brazil and Australasian tree ferns. Rhododendrons and hydrangeas lead to a private beach on the River Helford. ✆ *Map C5 • Mawnan Smith • 01326 252200 • Open 10am–dusk daily • Adm; half price for bus arrivals • www.trebahgarden.co.uk*

5 Tresco Abbey Gardens

First planted in 1834, these gardens, located in the Isles of Scilly, have been carefully nurtured by five generations of the same family. The region's climate, the mildest in the UK, has made it possible to cultivate exotic plants from around the southern hemisphere. The Tresco Abbey ruins are an evocative backdrop to the lush gardens *(see pp22–3)*.

The jungle in the Lost Gardens of Heligan

A stunning flower border at Rosemoor

Mount Edgcumbe

On the Rame Peninsula outside Plymouth, Mount Edgcumbe has Italian, French and American formal gardens and is home to the national camellia collection, which flowers from January. The parklands include follies and a deer park *(see p15)*.

Glendurgan

This wooded valley garden on the banks of the Helford has walled areas and herbaceous growths with brilliant colour and foliage. The spring-flowering magnolias and camellias are especially impressive. Children will enjoy the baffling laurel maze dating from 1833 and the Giant's Stride rope swing. ⊗ *Map C5 • Mawnan Smith • 01326 252020 • Open mid-Feb–Jul & Sep–Oct: 10:30am–5:30pm or dusk Tue–Sat; Aug: daily • Adm • www. nationaltrust.org.uk*

Rosemoor

In North Devon's Torridge Valley, RHS Rosemoor holds year-round interest, with snowdrops in winter, rhododendrons in spring, flower borders in summer and fiery hues in autumn. The most spectacular displays, however, are 2,000 roses with over 200 cultivars. Model gardens and woodland walks provide further interest. ⊗ *Map H2 • Great Torrington • 01805 624067 • Open Apr–Sep: 10am–6pm daily; Oct–Mar: 10am–5pm daily • Adm, RHS members free • www.rhs.org.uk*

Lanhydrock

Surrounding this grand manor house are horticultural spectacles, including a unique yew-hedged herbaceous garden, at its best in summer. Other highlights are magnolias from Sikkim, Tibet and southern China, hybrid rhododendrons and geraniums *(see pp8–9)*.

Bicton Park

This extensive estate has formal parterres of bedding plants and a renowned collection of trees, including a giant Grecian Fir. The elegant Palm House, dating from the 1820s, holds rare palms, while the Tropical House features the Bicton orchid. A woodland railway provides scenic rides through the landscaped park *(see p78)*.

The Royal Horticultural Society (RHS) is the world's leading horticultural body and the UK's biggest gardening charity.

Left **Prideaux Place** Right **Pencarrow House**

🔟 Great Houses

1 Trerice
An architectural gem with ornate fireplaces and elaborate ceilings, this small Elizabethan manor has a good collection of English furniture, clocks and examples of needlework. The highlight is the barrel ceiling of its Great Chamber. Tudor Costume Days are a popular attraction *(see p86)*.

2 Pencarrow
This 18th-century mansion is noted for its porcelain and paintings, including portraits by Joshua Reynolds *(see p57)*. The bedrooms upstairs display costumes used in films shot here. The gardens are home to the earliest Monkey Puzzle tree and rock garden in England *(see p83)*.

3 Cotehele House
Hidden in the byways of the Tamar Valley, this Tudor palace is a must for all fans of embroidery, with the bedrooms adorned in heavy tapestries – the absence of electric lights has helped to preserve these. The house also has four-poster beds and finely crafted furniture. It is best to visit on a sunny day *(see p93)*.

4 Prideaux Place
The Prideaux family has occupied this fine manor house since 1592. It holds many treasures, including loot from the Spanish Armada and the country's oldest cast-iron cannon. The grounds include a deer park, a grotto and a 9th-century Celtic cross *(see p30)*.

5 Hartland Abbey
This abbey, founded in 1157, was the last one in England to fall victim to the Dissolution of the Monasteries *(see p34)*, and has since been a private home. Today, its architecture and decoration range from medieval to Victorian-Gothic. Highlights include the vaulted Alhambra

Lanhydrock Garden

Corridor and the Regency library, which has portraits by Gainsborough and Reynolds.

🟡 Map G2 • Hartland, Bideford • 01237 441234 • Open Apr–Sep: 2–5pm Sun–Thu; grounds open at 11:30am • Adm • www.hartlandabbey.com

Buckland Abbey
Founded as a Cistercian abbey in 1278, Buckland Abbey was dissolved by Henry VIII, converted into a private home by the distinguished mariner Richard Grenville and acquired by Francis Drake in 1580. Drake's seafaring exploits are related here and visitors can admire the Great Barn, which is bigger than the house itself *(see p77)*.

Saltram
The grandiose exterior of this 18th-century mansion set in parkland outside Plymouth is matched by the succession of stately rooms inside, each decorated with a dazzling array of art. The most opulent is the Great Drawing Room, designed by Robert Adam *(see p14)*.

St Michael's Mount
This rocky island was linked with Normandy's Mont St Michel until 1424 and later became a fortified private home. The best-preserved parts are the Chevy Chase Room, the 14th-century church and the Lady Chapel, later converted into a drawing room *(see pp28–9)*.

Knightshayes Court
The original designer of this Victorian country pile was flamboyant architect William Burges. When

The dining room at Hartland Abbey

costs began to rocket, Burges was sacked, but enough of his Gothic-style interiors remain, including in the library, vaulted hall and the arched red drawing room. 🟡 Map K3 • Bolham, Tiverton • 01884 254665 • Open Feb & Mar: 11am–4pm daily; Apr–Oct: closes 5pm; Nov & Dec: 11am–4pm Wed–Sun; garden: open daily • Adm • www.nationaltrust.org.uk

Lanhydrock
This 17th-century palace was rebuilt in the High Victorian style after a fire in 1881, but the North Wing containing the Jacobean Long Gallery and the gatehouse survived. The building is filled with accoutrements of a 19th-century mansion, including the elaborate kitchens *(see pp8–9)*.

Left **National Seal Sanctuary** Centre **A model ship at Land's End** Right **A tamarin, Newquay Zoo**

Children's Attractions

National Seal Sanctuary

In this rescue centre, watch recovered and orphaned seals frolic in outdoor pools. Children will be charmed by the seal pups. Sometimes there are dolphins and turtles and the centre also cares for otters, ponies, goats and penguins. Feeding times and talks are popular daily events *(see p100)*.

Flambards

Attractions here include a recreated Victorian Village, where 50 shops and cottages are on show, and Britain in the Blitz. Thrills are provided by the Hornet Roller Coaster and the Canyon River Log Flume, while Hands on Science offers interactive fun. Fireworks are set off on Wednesday evenings in August. *Map B5 • Helston • 01326 573404 • Open Apr–Oct: 10am–5pm daily (last entry at 3pm); opening times vary when rides are closed, check website for details • Adm • www.flambards.co.uk*

Babbacombe Model Village

Children will love this miniature, all-weather world which includes railways, a model castle with a fire-breathing dragon and a 4D theatre. After dusk, 10,000 bulbs light up the streets, homes and gardens. *Map K5 • Hampton Ave, Babbacombe, Torquay • 01803 315315 • Opening times vary, check website for details • Adm • www.babbacombe modelvillage.co.uk*

The Monkey Sanctuary

This charitable sanctuary overlooking Looe Bay promotes the welfare of South American woolly and capuchin monkeys. A colony of lesser horseshoe bats housed here can be observed via cameras and infrared lights. The eco-friendly Tree Top Café offers delicious vegetarian food. *Map E4 • St Martin's, Looe • 01503 262532, 08442 721271 • Open Apr–Oct: 11am–4:30pm Sun–Thu • Adm • www.monkeysanctuary.org*

Miniature houses, Babbacombe Model Village

The best time to see seal pups is in autumn and winter.

Newquay Zoo

Cornwall's only zoo is set in lakeside gardens and is home to lions, lynxes, meerkats and tortoises. Fun activities for kids include exploring the Tarzan Trail and the Dragon Maze. Special events take place through the year *(see p83)*.

Paignton Zoo

Gorillas and gibbons are among the highlights at this zoo. Many animals can be viewed from the Jungle Express miniature railway. Recreated environments include the Crocodile Swamp, which is home to a variety of crocodiles *(see p78)*.

Land's End

Located at mainland Britain's most westerly point, this theme park offers audiovisual exhibitions, including a 4D film. At the interactive Arthur's Quest, visitors can seek the dragon in its fiery lair. Kids can get close to the animals at Greeb Farm. ✪ *Map A5 • Sennen • 08717 20044 • Open mid-Mar–Nov: 10am–4pm daily • Adm • www.landsend-landmark.co.uk*

Watermouth Castle

This Victorian folly castle and adventure park includes a model railway, water gardens and a Snake Tube Slide. The castle itself displays suits of armour and a 1950s organ on which life-size figures play instruments. Beware of the expensive slot machines in the dungeons. ✪ *Map H1 • Berrynarbor, Ilfracombe • 01271 867474 • Opening times vary, check website for details • Adm • www.watermouthcastle.com*

Lizard Lighthouse Heritage Centre

Lizard Lighthouse Heritage Centre

The lighthouse is now automated but in its visitor centre you can learn about working and living on a lighthouse. Visitors can sound a foghorn, track ships and even send messages in Morse code. Kids should be able to climb the stairs of the towers unaided *(see p100)*.

Living Coasts

Focusing on the conservation of coastal and marine life, this aquatic zoo features the flora and fauna that are found along Britain's coasts. Visitors can learn about a range of birds and mammals and the ecological issues affecting them. Living exhibits include avocets, puffins and cormorants, though the Penguin Beach and Fur Seal Cove are perennial favourites *(see p75)*.

Left **Museum of Barnstaple and North Devon** Right **Wayside Museum and Trewey Mill**

TOP 10 Museums

1 Overbeck's Museum
Scientist Otto Overbeck lived in this house until 1937. Many of his eccentric inventions, such as a "rejuvenating machine", share space with exhibits on local history. The garden has exotic plants and offers superb coastal views (see p78).

2 Royal Cornwall Museum
Cornwall's county museum addresses local geology and culture, with collections of insects on display alongside Roman coins found in the area. Buddhist figures from Burma and an unwrapped Egyptian mummy are also on show (see p91).

3 Museum of Dartmoor Life
Housed in a former granary, this museum illustrates aspects of the moor and its inhabitants, from prehistoric hut-dwellers to the tin-mining communities (see p12).

National Marine Aquarium

Trewinnard coach, Royal Cornwall Museum

4 Royal Albert Memorial Museum
Among the displays at Exeter's largest museum are items such as clocks and silverware, for which Exeter was well known. Sladen's study, named after the echinoderm expert, contains one of the largest collections of starfish and sea urchins in the world (see p19).

5 Wayside Museum and Trewey Mill
This eclectic jumble of memorabilia is like a scrapbook of West Cornwall life. Exhibits include pestles and mortars from 3,000 BC, a reconstructed Victorian parlour and displays illustrating occupations such as fishing, mining and smuggling. Copious cuttings and photographs provide a fascinating background (see p100).

6 National Marine Aquarium
Part traditional aquarium and part 21st-century museum, this complex offers an awe-inspiring survey of ocean life. Over 50 live exhibits contain some 4,000 examples of marine life (see p14).

7 Museum of Barnstaple and North Devon
This museum is the perfect place to learn about North Devon's history. Exhibits include locally minted

Display at the National Maritime Museum

Saxon coins, a 17th-century kiln and local pottery. The region's natural history is well represented and part of the museum is devoted to local militaria *(see p68)*.

National Maritime Museum, Cornwall

This museum displays boats from around the world, nautical equipment, interactive displays and marine art. The centrepiece is the grand Flotilla Gallery, where small craft hang from the roof *(see p100)*.

Fairlynch Museum

Fossils, prehistoric flints, 18th-century costumes, and collections of lace and toys at this museum help to create a picture of life in South Devon through the ages. The building is a fascinating exhibit in itself – a thatched *cottage orné* built by a local shipowner *(see p78)*.

Helston Folk Museum

This museum focuses on the social history of Helston and the Lizard Peninsula. It has sections dedicated to costume, telegraphy pioneer Marconi and the locally born boxing champion Bob Fitzsimmons (1863–1917). 🅂 *Map B5 • Market Place, Helston • 01326 564027 • Open 10am–4pm Mon–Sat • www.helstonmuseum.co.uk*

Top 10 Art Galleries

1 Tate St Ives
Absorb past and present artistic trends at this seaside gallery *(see p26)*.

2 The Exchange
The latest addition to the Penzance art scene *(see p28)*.

3 Newlyn Art Gallery
View modern works of art at this old fishing port. 🅂 *Map A5 • New Road, Newlyn • 01736 363715 • www.newlynartgallery.co.uk*

4 Burton Art Gallery and Museum
Paintings and prized local slipware are exhibited here. *(see p67)*.

5 Barbara Hepworth Museum and Sculpture Garden
View sculptures in Hepworth's beautiful garden *(see p26)*.

6 St Ives Society of Artists Gallery
This private gallery shows rotating exhibitions of local artists' work *(see p26)*.

7 Broomhill Sculpture Gardens
Part hotel and restaurant, part gallery and sculpture garden showing contemporary works. 🅂 *Map H2 • Muddiford Rd, Barnstaple • 01271 850262 • Adm • www.broomhillart.co.uk*

8 Falmouth Art Gallery
A strong collection of works by artists with local links *(see p100)*. • *www.falmouthartgallery.com*

9 Penlee House
The best place to see paintings of the Newlyn School *(see p28)*.

10 Exeter Phoenix
Three galleries of local and contemporary art. 🅂 *Map P2 • Gandy St • 01392 667080 • www.exeterphoenix.org.uk*

Left **Sir Arthur Conan Doyle** Right **Agatha Christie**

Famous Writers

1 D H Lawrence

D H Lawrence spent the years 1915–17 in the remote village of Zennor with his wife Frieda. He loved the "high shaggy moor hills, and big sweep of lovely sea", but was forced to leave in the face of hostility. He later described his Cornish experiences in the novel *Kangaroo*.

2 Sir Arthur Conan Doyle

Dartmoor provided the inspiration for Conan Doyle's yarn *The Hound of the Baskervilles*, based on a number of local legends concerning supernatural black dogs that inhabited the remotest reaches of the moor.

3 Charles Causley

Along with John Betjeman, Causley is one of the best known 20th-century poets associated with Cornwall. He was born and brought up in Launceston, returning to live there in 1946. His work drew on hymns and ballads, and described Cornish life and legends.

4 R D Blackmore

Although he wrote a number of novels, Blackmore is remembered today only for his swash-buckling romance *Lorna Doone* (1869), set on Exmoor in the 17th century. Fans can visit scenes described in this tale of the evil Doone clan, including the Valley of the Rocks outside Lynmouth.

R D Blackmore

5 Agatha Christie

Born in Torquay, the "Mistress of Murder" spent much of her life in South Devon, particularly in Greenway, a grand mansion overlooking the River Dart. The settings of her country-house whodunits have a strong flavour of the area. Torquay Museum has a good exhibition devoted to her.

6 Thomas Hardy

For Hardy, Cornwall was "the region of dream and mystery". Although he is more associated with Dorset, it was at Boscastle on the North Cornwall coast that he worked as an architect and met his first wife, Emma. His novel *A Pair of Blue Eyes* is set there.

Max Gate in Dorset, Thomas Hardy's home

Daphne du Maurier

Sir Arthur Quiller-Couch

"Q" was a famed literary critic, poet and author. He set many of his tales in Fowey, which appeared as "Troy" in his books. Visitors to Fowey can see a memorial to Q on the Hall Walk *(see p36)*. He was Professor of English at Cambridge University.

Henry Williamson

The novelist and naturalist set his classic animal tale *Tarka the Otter* in the lush countryside of North Devon. The book has been the inspiration of the Tarka Trail, a recreational route around the Taw and Torridge rivers.

Winston Graham

All 12 of Graham's Poldark novels, written between 1945 and 2002, were set mainly around Perranporth, but also took in other parts of Cornwall including Mousehole and Lanhydrock. The books enjoyed great success as TV adaptations in the 1970s.

Daphne du Maurier

Having spent many childhood holidays in Cornwall, du Maurier eventually settled outside Fowey. Drawn to Cornwall's secluded creeks and the wild romance of the moors, she set some of her famous novels here – including *Rebecca* and *Jamaica Inn*. An annual literary festival includes her work *(see p38)*.

Top 10 Artists in Devon and Cornwall

1 Joshua Reynolds
Born and raised near Plymouth, Reynolds was one of the foremost portrait artists of the 18th century.

2 Elizabeth Forbes
Born in Canada in 1859, the Newlyn painter is best known for her portrayal of children.

3 Stanhope Forbes
Husband of Elizabeth Forbes, the Irish-born artist was a leading figure of the Newlyn school.

4 Norman Garstin
His most famous work, *The Rain It Raineth Everyday* (1889), is on display in Penlee House, Penzance.

5 Alfred Wallis
A simple fisherman "discovered" by the St Ives artists, Wallis is known for his naïve style.

6 Bernard Leach
A higly influential potter, Leach was based for a long time in St Ives.

7 Barbara Hepworth
The St Ives studio of this sculptor is now a gallery displaying her works.

8 Ben Nicholson
Barbara Hepworth's husband exerted great influence with his austere, abstract paintings.

9 Terry Frost
One of Britain's most prominent abstract painters, Terry Frost was based mainly in St Ives and Newlyn.

10 Patrick Heron
His highly coloured abstract works are typified by his giant stained-glass window in the Tate St Ives.

Left **Ship Inn**, Exeter Right **Exterior of the Mason's Arms**

Pubs

Ship Inn, Exeter
Steps away from Exeter Cathedral, this inn was once Sir Francis Drake's *(see p17)* local haunt. The nautical theme is strong with maps, knots and clay pipes. Simple meals are served in the low-ceilinged bar or the restaurant upstairs.
⊗ Map P2 • 1–3 Martins Lane, Exeter • 01392 272040

Tinners Arms
This historic pub dates from 1271 and is a fine place for a drink and a meal. There is a warming log fire in winter and it hosts live music on most Thursdays. Children are also welcome. D H Lawrence *(see p56)* stayed here when he came to live in Zennor *(see p102)*.

Blisland Inn
A traditional country pub on Bodmin Moor, the Blisland Inn has Toby jugs hanging from wooden beams and walls festooned with photographs. A wide variety of real ales and tasty food is available. ⊗ Map E3 • Blisland • 01208 850739

Ship Inn, Mousehole
This excellent inn stands right above the harbour in a tiny fishing village. The Tinners and Tribute ales and the fish pie are worth

A toby jug at the Blisland Inn

sampling. If you miss out on a seat with harbour views, sit in the tiny patio garden upstairs. Accommodation is available *(see p102)*.

Warren House Inn
The third-highest pub in England stands in solitary splendour on Dartmoor. It is a welcome sight to walkers, with two hearths – one that has reputedly been kept burning since 1845 – and good, inexpensive food. ⊗ Map J4 • 4 km (2 miles) NE of Postbridge, Dartmoor • 01822 880208

Blue Anchor Inn
One of the best pubs in the West, Blue Anchor Inn is worth going out of your way for its Spingo bitters. The building is a former monks' resthouse divided into many small rooms. The pub has friendly staff and manages a B&B next door *(see p102)*.

Ship Inn, Mousehole

Tinners Arms

7 The Sloop
One of Cornwall's oldest pubs, with characterful beams, benches and nooks, the Sloop is a popular St Ives haunt right on the harbour. It offers a fine range of real ales and decent pub fare. Punters spill out onto the cobbled harbourside in summer. ◈ *Map B5* • *St Ives* • *01736 796584*

8 Turk's Head
Said to be Penzance's oldest pub, Turk's Head dates from 1233 and has a maze of low-ceilinged rooms, a beer garden and a smugglers' tunnel leading to the harbour. Real ales include Skinner's and Sharp's. ◈ *Map B5* • *Chapel St, Penzance* • *01736 363093*

9 Mason's Arms
Located 10 minutes from the beach, this East Devon inn dispenses great locally brewed bitters and serves top-notch food, including local mussels and crab. You can sit outside under thatched table umbrellas too. Rooms are available. ◈ *Map M4* • *Branscombe, Devon* • *01297 680300*

10 Bridge Inn
The pink-walled, 16th-century Bridge Inn, with real ales and traditional trappings, is one of Devon's best. It is reputedly the only pub to have been graced by the queen in an official capacity, when she visited in 1998. ◈ *Map K4* • *Bridge Hill, Topsham* • *01392 873862*

For more pubs **See p102.**

Top 10 Local Breweries

1 Skinners
This Truro-based brewery features ales named after Cornish folk heroes, such as Betty Stogs.

2 St Austell
This is Cornwall's major brewer, whose traditional cask ales include the legendary HSD and Tribute.

3 Sharp's
The Cornish producer of such fine beers as Doom Bar, Cornish Coaster and Orchard.

4 Otter
A Honiton-based brewery which produces five regular beers and one winter ale available throughout Devon.

5 O'Hanlon's
Located in Devon, this small, specialist brewery produces award-winning cask and bottled beers.

6 Country Life
Bideford-based producer of ales such as Old Appledore, the light-coloured Pot Wallop and Country Bumpkin.

7 Spingo Ales
These famous brews is available only in Helston's Blue Anchor, in four distinctive varieties from 4.5 per cent to 6.5 per cent ABV.

8 Driftwood Spars Brewery
Award-winning microbrews from the Driftwood Spars brew-pub at St Agnes *(see p115)*.

9 Ales of Scilly
Scilly-based producer of Firebrand and Scuppered bitters, in addition to some seasonal beers.

10 Harbour Brewing Co.
A progressive Cornish microbrewery offering a range of innovative beers.

Left **Tavistock Pannier Market** Right **Cornwall Crafts Association**

🔟 Shopping

1 Totnes Elizabethan Market
Every Tuesday morning throughout summer, local traders don Tudor costumes for the Elizabethan market, which runs alongside an all-day crafts market. 🕲 *Map K5 • Civic Square, Totnes • 01803 863714 • Open May–Sep*

2 Barnstaple Pannier Market
A lively market is held daily until around 4pm in this purpose-built hall dating from 1855. Come for books, clothing, household goods, local produce, crafts and antiques *(see p69)*.

3 Devon Guild of Craftsmen
This consortium sells some of the best contemporary crafts made in the region, including ceramics, textiles, jewellery and furniture. Its base at the edge of Dartmoor holds regular exhibitions. 🕲 *Map K4 • Riverside Mill, Bovey Tracey • 01626 832223*

Devon Guild of Craftsmen

4 Darts Farm
From its launch as a farm shop, Darts has evolved into a whole shopping hub based around the concept of fresh, locally sourced food. On site is a food hall, butchers, deli, fish shed, cider works, a restaurant and health and beauty treatments. 🕲 *Map K4 • Topsham, Exeter • 01392 878200 • www.dartsfarm.co.uk*

5 Shops at Dartington
Set in the grounds of Dartington Hall, this complex sells craft items, kitchenware, farm foods and toys besides the glassware for which it is well known. Regular exhibitions and food tastings take place throughout the year. The site also holds a Cranks vegetarian café. 🕲 *Map J5 • Shinners Bridge, Dartington • 01803 847500 • www.dartington.org*

6 Tavistock Pannier Market
Tavistock's indoor market is open on most days of the week. It offers antiques and collectables (Tuesdays), crafts (Wednesdays and Thursdays), local produce (Fridays), mixed markets (first and third Saturday of the month) and a Victorian market (fourth Saturday). 🕲 *Map H4 • Tavistock • 01822 660046*

Devon Guild of Craftsmen

Duchy of Cornwall Nursery

Top 10 Things to Buy

1 Local Art
Buy local art at small galleries, which are to Devon and Cornwall what antique shops are to the Cotswolds.

2 Serpentine
A speciality of the Lizard Peninsula, this greenish rock is used to make a variety of local ornaments.

3 Fudge
Creamy and delicious flavoured fudge is available in almost all gift shops throughout the region.

4 Ice cream
Most resorts have at least one shop selling quality ice cream in a range of contemporary flavours.

5 Local Wine and Gin
West Country wines are among the country's finest, while Plymouth gin is internationally famous.

6 Fishermen's Apparel
Fishing smocks, caps and woolly jumpers make great mementos and souvenirs.

7 Crafts
Hand-crafted woodwork, jewellery, silverware and glassware are among the West's specialities.

8 Fresh Seafood
Experience the thrill of buying seafood directly from the harbour. It can usually be iced and packaged for the ride back home.

9 Surf Gear
All the major surf gear brands are represented at outlets in the surfing centres of Devon and Cornwall.

10 Pottery
Some of the country's most renowned potters are based in the West and exhibit their wares.

7 Duchy of Cornwall Nursery
One of the largest nurseries in the Southwest, this place is an inspiration to gardeners, offering a range of shrubs, ornamental and fruit trees, climbers and conservatory plants. Specialities include conifers, fuchsias, bamboos and camellias. *Map E4*
• *Cott Road, Lostwithiel* • *01208 872668*
• *www.duchyofcornwallnursery.co.uk*

8 Cornwall Crafts Association
A range of top quality Cornish arts and crafts are exhibited and sold at two locations. The goods give an idea of contemporary trends. *Trelowarren: Map B5; Mawgan-in-Meneage, Helston; 01326 221567* • *Trelissick Gardens: Map C5; Trelissick, Feock, Truro; 01872 864514*
• *www.cornwallcrafts.co.uk*

9 Bickleigh Mill
A working 18th-century watermill is the venue for this retail centre, which sells jewellery, ceramics and soaps, seasonal gifts and toys. *Map K3*
• *Bickleigh, Tiverton* • *01884 855419*
• *www.bickleighmill.com*

10 St Ives Art Galleries
St Ives is a magnet for art enthusiasts, not just for established names exhibited in the Tate and the myriad smaller galleries. Styles and quality vary, as do the prices *(see p26)*.

Left **A train on the Liskeard-to-Looe line** Right **The Paignton-Kingswear Railway line**

🔟 Great Train Rides

1 Exeter to Newton Abbot

From Exeter, the main line runs beside two estuaries, the Exe and the Teign, offering delightful vistas over the serene mudflats populated by wading birds. ⊗ *Map K4 • 08457 484950*

2 Tarka Line

Named after *Tarka the Otter*, which was largely set around here, this 65-km (39-mile) line, centred on Barnstaple, weaves through Devon's rural heartland. After Crediton, it sticks close to the River Taw, passing through woodlands inhabited by woodpeckers and buzzards. ⊗ *Map H1–H3 • 08457 484950*

3 Atlantic Coast Line

This 33-km (21-mile) coast-to-coast line runs from the English Channel at Par Station to Newquay on the Atlantic, passing through the lunar landscape of china clay country. ⊗ *Map C4–D4 • 08457 484950*

4 Bodmin and Wenford Railway

The steam or diesel engines of this private standard-gauge line provide an excellent way to explore the countryside around Bodmin. The terminus at Bodmin Parkway is linked by a 3-km (2-mile) path to Lanhydrock *(see pp8–9)*. There is direct access to the Camel Trail from Boscarne Junction and to Cardinham Woods from Colesloggett Halt. ⊗ *Map D4 • 01208 73555 • www.bodminrailway.co.uk*

5 Looe Valley Line

The fishing port of Looe is linked to Liskeard by this branch line dating from 1860. The route runs beside the river through the heavily wooded Looe Valley. ⊗ *Map E4 • 08457 484950*

6 Tamar Valley Line

This branch line meanders through the Tamar Valley. The highlight is the Calstock Viaduct

The Bodmin and Wenford Steam Railway

Check www.nationalrail.co.uk for train information, unless otherwise shown.

crossing between Devon and Cornwall. A "rail ale trail" is available for visiting pubs along the way. 🕲 Map F4 • 08457 484950

7 South Devon Railway

From a station outside Totnes, steam trains of the South Devon Railway depart several times daily, between April and October (and some dates in winter), for a scenic ride to Buckfastleigh, on the edge of Dartmoor. There is a stop at Staverton, with access to a path beside the River Dart (see p80).

8 Launceston Steam Railway

These narrow gauge steam engines from the Victorian era run for 4 km (3 miles) between Launceston and Newmills. At Launceston Station you can wander around the railway workshops, an engineering museum and the ruins of an Augustinian Priory. 🕲 Map F3 • 01566 775665
• www.launcestonsr.co.uk

9 Paignton and Dartmouth Steam Railway

This heritage line runs along the Tor Bay coast from Paignton Station before chugging alongside the River Dart to Kingswear. A "round robin" ticket includes a river cruise from Dartmouth to Totnes as well as a coach back to the town of Paignton. 🕲 Map K5 • 01803 555872
• www.dartmouthrailriver.co.uk

10 St Erth to St Ives

This picturesque branch line is the best way to reach St Ives (see pp26–7). It edges along the Hayle Estuary before winding around the beaches of St Ives Bay, ending up steps away from Porthminster Beach. 🕲 Map B5
• 08457 484950

Top 10 Beauty Spots

1 Lydford Gorge, Dartmoor

This lovely spot offers riverside walks, a whirlpool and a waterfall (see p13).

2 Hartland Point

Cliffs and crags flank this promontory with views of Lundy Island (see p70).

3 Roseland Peninsula

One of the region's most photogenic, least spoilt spots, with two waterside churches (see p91).

4 Valley of the Rocks, Exmoor

This dry valley has striking rock formations and coastal views (see p70).

5 Golitha Falls, Bodmin Moor

A series of waterfall cascades gush through oak and beech woodland. 🕲 Map E3

6 Lizard Point

A wild, rocky promontory at England's southern tip, with invigorating walks to beaches. 🕲 Map C6

7 Watersmeet, Exmoor

A canopy of oaks covers this confluence of the East Lyn and Hoar Oak rivers. Ideal for walks (see p70).

8 Cape Cornwall, Penwith Peninsula

The ocean pounds against this craggy headland, overlooked by an abandoned chimney stack. 🕲 Map A5

9 Dartmeet, Dartmoor

The West and East Dart rivers merge here, right by a "clapper" bridge and close to a nature reserve (see p13).

10 Hell Bay, Isles of Scilly

On the island of Bryher, this dramatic and stunning bay bears the full brunt of Atlantic storms. 🕲 Map A4

AROUND DEVON AND CORNWALL

DEVON AND CORNWALL'S TOP 10

Left **Museum of Barnstaple and North Devon** Right **Boat moored on the beach at Appledore**

North Devon

BETWEEN THE AUSTERE HEIGHTS OF EXMOOR *and the rocky pinnacles of Hartland Point, North Devon crams in a rich landscape. Two of the region's top nature reserves, Northam Burrows and Braunton Burrows, and some of the best beaches, such as Woolacombe Bay, Saunton Sands and Westward Ho! are located on this stretch of coast. The main towns are Barnstaple, Ilfracombe and Bideford, but the true treasures are the coastal villages of Appledore and Clovelly. Inland, the Tarka Trail is ideal for cycling or walking, while out at sea, Lundy Island is home to puffins and seals.*

Scenic Croyde Bay, near the town of Barnstaple

🔟 Sights

1. Tarka Trail
2. Woolacombe Bay
3. Braunton Burrows
4. Burton Art Gallery and Museum
5. Appledore
6. Clovelly
7. Museum of Barnstaple and North Devon
8. Lynton and Lynmouth
9. Barnstaple Pannier Market
10. Lundy Island

Preceding pages **The magnificent nave in Exeter Cathedral**

Surfers at Woolacombe Bay

Tarka Trail

Henry Williamson's classic animal fable *Tarka the Otter (see p68)* was set around his native North Devon. The otter's epic journeys are traced in this 300-km (180-mile) trail, which describes a figure of eight centring on the town of Barnstaple and incorporating sections of the South West Coast Path and the Tarka Line railway. Over 50 km (30 miles) of the trail, between Braunton and Meeth, can be cycled. Other sections take in the scenic Taw Valley and Williamson's home village of Georgeham.
✦ *Map H1–H3*

Woolacombe Bay

Surfers know this impressive arc of sand as one of the country's top sites for riding the waves, but non-surfers will find plenty of elbow room here, especially at the more sheltered southern end, Putsborough. Surf equipment can be rented at shops and stalls above the beach, where there are also a handful of cafés and bars.
✦ *Map H1*

Braunton Burrows

The core of a UN-designated biosphere, this wild and wind-blown area constitutes the largest sand-dune system in the UK. The dunes are stabilized by marram grass and a range of other plants. More than 400 recorded species of vascular plants and a great variety of invertebrate species make their home here. The area is traversed by meandering paths, and can be reached on the Tarka Trail and the South West Coast Path *(see pp36–7)*. ✦ *Map H2*

Burton Art Gallery and Museum

The "little white town" of Bideford, rich with historical associations and home of the Elizabethan mariner Sir Richard Grenville, houses the Burton Art Gallery and Museum. The gallery boasts an absorbing collection of art and artifacts including watercolours, model ships and replicas of the famed local slipware. The museum is located in Victoria Park, where cannons taken from the Spanish Armada are exhibited *(see p17)*. ✦ *Map H2*
• *Kingsley Road, Bideford* • *01237 471455*
• *Open 10am–5pm Mon–Fri, 10am–4pm Sat, 11am–4pm Sun; Oct–Jun: closes 4pm* • *www.burtonartgallery.co.uk*

Pottery at Burton Art Gallery and Museum

The settlement of Clovelly tumbling down to a small harbour

steep main street unmanageable. Some of the cottages are open to the public, including a museum dedicated to Charles Kingsley, author of *The Water Babies*, who lived here as a child. ◈ *Map G2 • Tourist information: 01237 431781 • www.clovelly.co.uk*

Appledore

A stately air hangs over this off-the-beaten-track settlement of Georgian houses at the edge of the Torridge Estuary. Behind the seafront, narrow lanes hold shops and pubs, leading uphill to the Maritime Museum with its collection of nautical items. The autumn Appledore Book Festival features well-known authors. For the best estuary views, a pint and tasty seafood, head for the two pubs on Irsha Street. ◈ *Map H2 • Maritime Museum: 01237 422064; open Apr–Oct: 10am–5pm daily • Adm • www.northdevonmaritimemuseum.co.uk*

Clovelly

This picturesque settlement clings to a steep cliff and plunges down to a small harbour. The town is privately owned and there is an absence of cars, except for a Land Rover service for visitors who find the

Museum of Barnstaple and North Devon

One of Devon's finest museums has a gloriously eclectic collection, including features on the area's wildlife and a gallery devoted to *Tarka the Otter*. You can walk through a model Wellington bomber, view fascinating timepieces and admire superbly crafted glassware. A highlight is the Barum Ware – startlingly original pottery for which the area is renowned. ◈ *Map H2 • The Square, Barnstaple • 01271 346747 • Open Apr–Oct: 10am–5pm Mon–Sat; Nov–Mar: 10am–4pm Mon–Sat*

Lynton and Lynmouth

These villages on the Exmoor coast, linked by a water-powered funicular, have drawn visitors since the 1800s when the poet Shelley spent his honeymoon here. Nestled among hills, the villages are

Tarka the Otter

North Devon's Tarka Line, Tarka Trail and Tarka Country all refer to *Tarka the Otter*, written by Henry Williamson. The book narrates the adventures of a young otter amid the beautiful landscape of North Devon – "the country of the two rivers". The book has retained its place as a classic animal tale, and was made into a film in 1979, narrated by Peter Ustinov.

The River Lyn flowing through Lynmouth

Visit www.northdevon.com, www.lynton-lynmouth-tourism.co.uk and www.staynorthdevon.co.uk for more information.

The Pannier Market, Barnstaple

a haven of tranquillity, though it was not always peaceful here. Lynmouth, by the sea, was devastated by a flash flood in 1952; the Glen Lyn Gorge, through which the torrent raged, holds an exhibition in memory of the event. ◎ Map J1

Barnstaple Pannier Market

This covered market in the town centre is the most famous of Devon's "pannier markets" – so called because traders originally brought their wares in baskets or panniers. The markets held here offer antiques, crafts, local produce, household items and clothes. Alongside is Butchers Row, which once held butchers' shops and is now home to a variety of stores selling clothes, antiques, household items and gifts. ◎ Map H2 • Butchers Row, Barnstaple • 01271 379084 • Open Mon–Sat • barnstaplepanniermarket.co.uk

Lundy Island

This remote 5-km (3-mile) long sliver of land is located north of Hartland Point. It gets its name from the puffins that inhabit the island (lunde is Norse for puffin). Unusual accommodation here includes a lighthouse and a radio room. ◎ Map G1 • Tourist information: 01271 863636 • www.lundyisland.co.uk

A Drive along the North Devon Coast

Morning

Begin your tour in the sister villages of **Lynton** and **Lynmouth** at the foot of Exmoor. The upper village, Lynton, is connected by an ingenious cliff railway to Lynmouth. From here it is a short drive to **Ilfracombe**, a cheerfully traditional resort with a bustling harbour. On the coast south of Ilfracombe, **Woolacombe** and **Croyde** beaches (see p41) invite a stopover. Though very different – Croyde is a sheltered inlet while Woolacombe is a long, curving bay – both are good for families as well as watersports enthusiasts. You can either indulge in a beachside picnic lunch or drive inland to lunch at the **Broomhill Art Hotel** (see p71), where the sculpture will prove absorbing.

Afternoon

In the afternoon, halt at Barnstaple, home to the lively **Pannier Market** as well as the interesting **Museum of Barnstaple and North Devon**. Alternatively, stop at Bideford for a visit to the **Burton Art Gallery and Museum**, which hosts regular exhibitions. Up at the mouth of the estuary, **Appledore** has another museum you can explore, but a stroll along the riverside is equally enjoyable. Proceed west along Bideford Bay to **Clovelly**, an enchanting, well-preserved village and stop for tea. If time allows, take a walk along **Hobby Drive** (see p36) or just continue west to **Hartland Abbey** (see p50), a majestic mansion with lovely grounds sweeping down to the sea.

Left **Watersmeet near Lynmouth** Right **The harbour at Clovelly**

🔟 Beauty Spots

Valley of the Rocks

West of Lynton, this steep heathland is dominated by rugged rock formations. Herds of wild goats still roam free as they have done here for centuries. ◎ *Map J1*

Watersmeet

In a deep wooded gorge, Hoar Oak Water joins with the East Lyn River on its way down to the sea. Shady riverside walks branch out from here. ◎ *Map J1*

Hartland Point

On Devon's northwestern tip, overlooked by a solitary lighthouse, this remote, storm-battered headland has dramatic coastal views of slate cliffs, jagged black rocks and swirling sea. ◎ *Map G2*

Clovelly

There is no denying the loveliness of this village, with its neat cottages and miniature harbour *(see p68)*.

Saunton Sands

The first view of this 6-km (3-mile) westward-facing strand is breathtaking, with ranks of Atlantic rollers advancing in a stately procession. This spot is a favourite among surfers. ◎ *Map H2*

Lynmouth

The East and West Lyn rivers flow placidly into the sea at this cliff-sheltered Exmoor village.

The Glen Lyn Gorge has woodland walks and waterfalls *(see p68)*.

Northam Burrows

Located next to Westward Ho!, this expanse of grasslands, salt marsh and sand dunes offers wonderful views across the Taw/ Torridge Estuary. The broad beach in front attracts surfers and sail-boarders. ◎ *Map H2*

Weare Giffard

This graceful village in the wooded Torridge Valley boasts a 15th-century manor house and a weathered pub. It is accessible from the Tarka Trail. ◎ *Map H2*

Hillsborough

Outside Ilfracombe, the summit of this 136-m (447-ft) hill is one of the few places in the country where you can see the sun rise and set over the sea. ◎ *Map H1*

Lundy Island

This remote outpost where the Atlantic meets the Bristol Channel is either utterly tranquil or in complete uproar, depending on the sea *(see p69)*.

Price Categories

For a three-course meal for one with half a bottle of wine, including taxes and extra charges.	**£** under £20
	££ £20–£35
	£££ £35–£45
	££££ £45–£55
	£££££ over £55

Red Lion pub, Clovelly

Places to Eat

1 Broomhill Art Hotel
This unusual place houses the relaxed Terra Madre restaurant where the emphasis is on local seasonal produce presented in modern style. Bar meals are also available. ⊗ *Map H2 • Muddiford Rd, Barnstaple • 01271 850262 • Open Wed–Sun lunch, Wed–Sat dinner (booking advised) • ££*

2 The Quay
This fashionable harbourside eatery, co-owned by artist Damien Hirst, features a menu that mixes Mediterranean and British cooking. ⊗ *Map H1 • 11 The Quay, Ilfracombe • 01271 868090 • £££*

3 Fremington Quay Café
This café is an ideal stop for those exploring the Tarka Trail from Barnstaple to Bideford. It serves drinks, cakes, cream teas and lunch with an emphasis on local ingredients. ⊗ *Map H2 • Fremington Quay, Barnstaple • 01271 268720 • £*

4 Red Lion
Right on the harbour, this hotel-restaurant offers great views. Local fish and meat dominate the menu. ⊗ *Map G2 • Clovelly • 01237 431237 • £££*

5 Mariners
A short walk from the quay, this eatery serves food prepared using local ingredients and fresh vegetables. A good place to try some fresh fish. ⊗ *Map F1 • 4 Cooper St, Bideford • 01237 476447 • Closed Oct–Mar: Sun–Tue • £££*

6 Rising Sun
Right on the harbour, this 14th-century inn claims to have once accommodated the poet Shelley. Enjoy the British-style cuisine in an atmospheric setting. ⊗ *Map J1 • Harbourside, Lynmouth • 01598 753223 • ££*

7 The Boathouse
This popular beachside eatery offers classics like fish pie and lasagne along with specials of the day such as lobster, crab and prawns. ⊗ *Map H2 • Marine Parade, Instow • 01271 861292 • ££*

8 Marisco Tavern
Lundy's sole pub dishes up island specialities of lamb and meat from Soay sheep and venison from Sika deer. ⊗ *Map G1 • Lundy Island • 01237 431831 • ££*

9 La Gendarmerie
Housed in a former police station, La Gendarmerie offers options like "nose to tail" pork and Lundy lobster. You can see the chef at work in his open kitchen. ⊗ *Map H1 • 63 Fore St, Ilfracombe • 01271 865984 • Closed summer: lunch & Mon, winter: Sun–Tue • £££*

10 Watersmeet House
At a famous Exmoor beauty spot, this Victorian fishing lodge is now a tea room and garden where you can enjoy refreshments before or after exploring the river banks. ⊗ *Map J1 • Watersmeet Rd, Lynmouth • 01598 753348 • Open daytime in mid-Mar–Oct • £*

For more restaurants in the region **See pp81, 87, 95 and 103.**

Left **The Choir, Exeter Cathedral** Right **The Promenade, Plymouth**

South Devon

A GENTEEL AURA PERVADES MUCH OF SOUTH DEVON. *Verdant meadows are interspersed with cob-and-thatch villages and rivers drift serenely through wooded valleys dotted with tidy cottages. Crumbly red cliffs rear above beaches, while in the forbidding expanse of Dartmoor, lonely tors gaze over slopes of bracken and gorse, and isolated communities huddle around centuries-old churches. A world away from these rural scenes are Exeter and Plymouth, the historic power centres, with their scattering of medieval and Elizabethan remains.*

Sights

1 Powderham Castle
2 A La Ronde
3 Living Coasts
4 Exeter
5 Church of the Holy Cross
6 Lydford Gorge
7 Plymouth
8 Torre Abbey Mansion
9 Buckland Abbey
10 Dartmoor

A thatched cottage, Dartmoor National Park

Preceding pages **The view from a tor on Dartmoor**

1 Powderham Castle

Surrounded by a deer park, this stately pile is the long-time seat of the earls of Devon and featured in the film *Remains of the Day*. Tours allow you to view the ornate music room, the majestic dining room, lavish bedrooms and the Victorian kitchen.

Powderham Castle

Kids will love the stories of ghosts, the secret door and the activity trails in the grounds.
Ⓢ *Map K4 • Kenton • 01626 890243*
• Open Apr–Oct: 11am–4:30pm Sun–Fri
• Adm • www.powderham.co.uk

2 A La Ronde

When the Parminter cousins, Jane and Mary, returned from their European travels in 1790, they brought with them trunk-loads of souvenirs and a unique vision. They built this 16-sided house which they filled with their mementos and creations. These ranged from seaweed and sand concoctions to a frieze made of game-bird and chicken feathers, and a shell-covered gallery.
Ⓢ *Map L4 • Summer Lane, Exmouth*
• 01395 265514 • Open Mar–Oct: 11am–5pm daily • Adm • www. nationaltrust.org.uk

The Living Coasts exhibition

3 Living Coasts

This informative aquatic exhibition focuses mainly on the coastlines of the world. The accurately reconstructed beaches, cliff faces and an estuary illustrate the diverse wildlife. Spot cormorants, penguins and puffins in an aviary, and South American fur seals in the seal cove. The waterside café offers wonderful views of Tor Bay. Ask about discounted tickets if you are also visiting Paignton Zoo *(see p78)*. Ⓢ *Map K5 • Beacon Quay, Torquay • 01803 202470, 08444 743366 • Open 10am–dusk daily • Adm • www.livingcoasts.org.uk*

4 Exeter

Devon's capital is a relaxed place with a historic core that includes the region's oldest cathedral and a treasure trove of a museum. Other attractions include a network of underground passages, historic civic and religious buildings and the old quayside area. The city has an active cultural life, with a year-round programme of festivals and events, and a good selection of theatres and restaurants. The Princesshay complex offers the region's best shopping opportunities and a range of restaurants and cafés. Enquire at the city's tourist office about walking tours *(see pp18–19)*.

Church of the Holy Cross

This red sandstone structure from around the 15th century is one of Devon's grandest churches. It stands on the site initially occupied by a monastery church, which was founded by the great missionary St Boniface. Born in Crediton around AD 680, he went on to become patron saint of Germany and the Netherlands. Brightly illuminated by large windows, the church building is full of historical interest. Its Lady Chapel is thought to have provided the model for the one in Exeter Cathedral.

⊗ Map K3 • Church St, Crediton • 01363 773226

Church of the Holy Cross

Lydford Gorge

On the edge of Dartmoor, the River Lyd thunderously gushes through this steep, oak-wooded ravine, home to the spectacular Devil's Cauldron whirlpool and the White Lady Waterfall that plummets 28 m (90 ft). There are walking opportunities along the river and a winding upper path

but come prepared with robust boots to navigate the trickier parts. Children must be supervised and access may be difficult for those with mobility problems *(see pp12–13)*.

Plymouth

This historic city, closely associated with Sir Francis Drake, rewards prolonged exploration. Remnants of the Elizabethan city survive, notably in the harbourside Barbican quarter. Other attractions that merit a visit include the beguiling National Marine Aquarium and the Plymouth Gin Distillery. Don't miss the magnificent sea views from Plymouth Hoe, a high, grassy esplanade. Bus and walking tours are available all year *(see pp14–15)*.

Torre Abbey Mansion

One of Devon's greatest museums is housed in a mansion house converted from abbey buildings after the Dissolution of the Monasteries in 1539 *(see p34)*. The collection is strong in 19th-century art, including works by Holman Hunt and Burne-Jones. The grounds have medieval ruins and a tithe

White Lady falls, Lydford Gorge

Dartmoor ponies – a mother and her foal

barn – known as the "Spanish Barn" after it was used to hold prisoners from the Spanish Armada. Temporary exhibitions and cultural events are held here. ⊛ Map K5 • King's Drive, Torquay • 01803 293593 • www.torre-abbey.org.uk

Buckland Abbey

The former home of Elizabethan mariners Richard Grenville and Francis Drake, this handsome manor house is positioned in beautiful grounds in the Tavy Valley. Visitors can look round the monastic Great Barn, Elizabethan Garden and the Abbey, where galleries feature interactive displays. Exhibits include Drake's Drum which, according to legend, will sound when England is in danger to summon Drake from his grave. ⊛ Map H5 • Yelverton • 01822 853607 • Open mid-Mar–Oct: 10:30am–5:30pm daily; Nov: Fri–Sun; Dec & Feb: daily • Adm • www.nationaltrust.org.uk

Dartmoor

In a region dominated by the sea, Dartmoor is a windy wasteland where semi-wild ponies roam. Many prehistoric remains lie scattered across the moor, while on its edges are market towns Okehampton and Tavistock. This area demands active exploration, with opportunities for caving, walking, canoeing and wildlife watching. (see pp12–13).

A Driving Tour in South Devon

Morning

Start from the fishing village of **Beer** (see p79), associated with the infamous exploits of smuggler Jack Rattenbury, located close to the Dorset border. You can grab a crab sandwich on the beach. Follow the A3052 east to **Sidmouth** (see p79), whose seafront and Esplanade are ideal for a stroll. The town is studded with well-preserved villas from the Regency period. The museum includes a lovely display of lace. Indulge in a good seaside lunch at Sidmouth.

Afternoon

Further west, just outside **Exmouth** (see p79) off the A376, stop to admire **A La Ronde** (see p75), a remarkable 16-sided folly constructed by cousins Jane and Mary Parminter. Continue to the M5, then take the A380 and A381 south to **Totnes** (see p79). Despite its hippy vibe, the town retains much of its Elizabethan character and has a Norman castle and a 14th-century church. The town's tearooms offer tasty refreshments. From Totnes, drive or take a river cruise down the River Dart to the sailing resort of **Dartmouth** (see p79), also filled with mementos from the Elizabethan era. From Totnes or Dartmouth, it is an easy excursion to the South Hams, an area of sleepy villages and soothing views. Unless you are based in Totnes or Dartmouth, either stay over in Kingsbridge or Salcombe, or head back up the A381 to **Exeter** (see pp18–19).

Left **Fairlynch Museum** Right **Bicton Park**

1 Fairlynch Museum
This 19-century *cottage orné* houses a collection of local memorabilia including lace, costumes and toys. ⊗ *Map L4 • 27 Fore St, Budleigh Salterton • 01395 442666 • Open Apr–Sep: 2–4:30pm Tue–Sun*

2 Beer Quarry Caves
These caves have been in use since Roman times for quarrying Beer stone. ⊗ *Map M4 • Quarry Lane, Beer • 01297 680282 • Open Apr–Sep: 10am–5pm, Oct: 10am–4pm • Adm • www.beerquarrycaves.co.uk*

3 Burgh Island
This tiny isle can be reached in high tide by sea tractor. Once there, you can stay in the luxurious Burgh Island Hotel *(see p114).* ⊗ *Map J6 • Bigbury-on-Sea*

4 Overbeck's Museum
A quirky collection gathered by inventor Otto Overbeck is housed in this museum. ⊗ *Map J6 • Sharpitor, Salcombe • 01548 842893 • Open mid-Feb–Oct: 11am–5pm daily • Adm • www.nationaltrust.org.uk*

5 Paignton Zoo
This zoo is designed to mimic the natural habitats of the animals that live here. ⊗ *Map K5 • Totnes Rd, Paignton • 08444 742222 • Open 10am–6pm (closes 5pm in winter) • Adm • www.paigntonzoo.org.uk*

6 Bicton Park
This horticultural idyll includes a formal garden reputedly inspired by Versailles in the 1730s and a Palm House from the 1820s. ⊗ *Map L4 • East Budleigh, Budleigh Salterton • 01395 568465 • Open summer: 10am–6pm; winter: closes 4:30pm • Adm • www.bictongardens.co.uk*

7 Allhallows Museum
Housed in the oldest building in town, this museum displays fine lace. ⊗ *Map L3 • High St, Honiton • 01404 44966 • Open Apr–Oct • Adm • www.honitonmuseum.co.uk*

8 Kingsbridge Cookworthy Museum
The museum is named after the pioneer of hard-paste English porcelain made from china clay. ⊗ *Map J6 • 108 Fore St, Kingsbridge • 01548 853235 • Open Apr–Oct • Adm*

9 Berry Head, Torbay
This site is home to guillemots and the endangered Greater Horseshoe Bat. ⊗ *Map K5*

10 Blackpool Sands
This is one of South Devon's premier beaches, home to the renowned Venus Café. ⊗ *Map K6 • Near Dartmouth • www.blackpoolsands. co.uk*

Left **Salcombe** Centre **Boats at Budleigh Salterton** Right **Branscombe**

Towns and Villages

Salcombe
1 At the mouth of the placid Kingsbridge Estuary, Devon's southernmost port is a magnet for sailors. Beaches, coastal walks and Overbeck's Museum are all nearby. ❧ *Map J6*

Sidmouth
2 The queen of East Devon resorts, elegant Sidmouth has a long Esplanade fronted by a shingle strand, though families prefer Jacob's Ladder, a more secluded beach to the west. ❧ *Map L4*

Totnes
3 The age of this riverside town is attested by its Norman castle and medieval remains. It is popular with craftworkers and has some fine glassware. ❧ *Map K5*

Cockington
4 There is no denying the rustic appeal of this well-preserved village, a calm contrast to the ebullience of neighbouring Torquay. ❧ *Map K5*

Brixham
5 Much of the seafood served in the region's restaurants is landed at this harbour. A replica of the *Golden Hind*, the vessel in which Francis Drake circumnavigated the globe, is moored here. ❧ *Map K5*

Beer
6 The village is best known for fishing, smuggling and Beer stone, a prized building material. A culvert carries a stream along the main street, from where you descend to the beach. ❧ *Map M4*

Dartmouth
7 The Royal Regatta and the Royal Naval College confirm this port's yachting credentials. Impressive Tudor buildings and a castle add to its allure. ❧ *Map K6*

Budleigh Salterton
8 John Millais painted his famous *Boyhood of Raleigh* on the pebble beach of this village. The Fairlynch Museum here is well worth a wander. ❧ *Map L4*

Exmouth
9 Primarily a family resort, Exmouth gets quite lively during the summer. The Beacon, an elegant row overlooking the sea, once accommodated the wives of Byron and Nelson. ❧ *Map L4*

Torquay
10 Capital of the so-called English Riviera, engaging Torquay, with its palms and fairy lights, smacks unmistakably of the Mediterranean. ❧ *Map K5*

Left **St Mary's** Centre **South Devon Railway** Right **Buckfast Abbey**

🔟 Sights Along the River Dart

1 Buckfast Abbey
The River Dart flows out of Dartmoor through the grounds of this Benedictine house. The few monks still living here are famed for their tonic wine. 🔍 *Map J5 • Buckfastleigh • 01364 645500 • Open 9am–6pm Mon–Sat, noon–6pm Sun • www.buckfast.org.uk*

2 Elizabethan Museum
This museum, in a cloth merchant's home that was built in 1575, has a room devoted to Totnes-born mathematician Charles Babbage, who built the forerunner of the computer. 🔍 *Map K5 • 70 Fore St, Totnes • 01803 863821 • Open Apr–Sep: 10:30am–4pm Mon–Sat • Adm*

3 St Mary's
This red sandstone building boasts a rood-screen of delicate tracery dating from 1460. 🔍 *Map K5 • High St, Totnes • 01803 840113*

4 The Guildhall
Built on the ruins of a priory in 1553, Guildhall later housed a courtroom and jail cells. It displays a table said to have been used by Oliver Cromwell *(see pp18–19)*.

5 South Devon Railway
Travel back in time in a Great Western Railway coach hauled by a steam locomotive. The line follows the Dart between Totnes and Buckfastleigh. 🔍 *Map J5 • Station Rd, Buckfastleigh • 08433 571420 • Open mid-Mar–Oct • Adm • www.southdevonrailway.co.uk*

6 Riverlink Cruises
The most relaxing way to explore the Dart is a cruise between Totnes and Dartmouth, which takes about an hour and a half. 🔍 *Map K5 • 5 Lower St, Dartmouth • 01803 555872 • Times vary • Adm • www.dartmouthrailriver.co.uk*

7 Greenway
Agatha Christie's private holiday home, furnished in 1950s style, is full of her family's collections of books, china and more. Car parking must be pre-booked. 🔍 *Map J6 • Galmpton, Devon • 01803 842382 • Open Mar–Dec: times vary • Adm • www.nationaltrust.org.uk*

8 Dartmouth Museum
A great collection of maritime models and other items relating to Dartmouth is housed in this merchant's house. 🔍 *Map K5 • Duke St, Dartmouth • 01803 832923 • Open Apr–Oct: 10am–4pm Tue–Sat, 1–4pm Sun & Mon; Nov–Mar: noon–3pm daily • Adm • www.dartmouthmuseum.org*

9 Dartmouth Royal Regatta
Pomp and pageantry are the order of the day at this annual jamboree celebrating the port's maritime traditions. 🔍 *Map K5 • 01803 834912 (Regatta period only) • Aug end • www.dartmouthregatta.co.uk*

10 Dartington Hall
Founded by US heiress Dorothy Elmhirst, this arts and education centre hosts a range of cultural events. 🔍 *Map J5 • 01803 847070 • www.dartington.org*

There are a variety of ways to travel to Greenway, including by ferry, vintage bus and steam train.

Price Categories

For a three-course meal for one with half a bottle of wine (or equivalent meal), taxes and extra charges.

£	under £20
££	£20–£35
£££	£35–£45
££££	£45–£55
£££££	over £55

Left **Michael Caines at Abode** Right **Horn of Plenty**

🔟 Places to Eat

1 Horn of Plenty
This Georgian house in the Tamar Valley serves creative British cuisine. Monday's pot-luck menu is cheaper but offers less choice, though the quality is guaranteed. ⊗ *Map H4 • Gulworthy, Dartmoor • 01822 832528 • £££££*

2 Gidleigh Park
Noted chef Michael Caines has garnered two Michelin stars for his original interpretations of modern European cuisine at this luxurious hotel-restaurant. Reservations are essential. ⊗ *Map J4 • Chagford • 01647 432367 • £££££*

3 Dartmoor Inn
Indulge in imaginatively prepared Mediterranean and British dishes at this gastro-pub. The cosy dining areas have open fires and wood or stone floors. ⊗ *Map H4 • Lydford • 01822 820221 • Closed Mon lunch & Sun dinner • £££*

4 Michael Caines at Abode
This spacious restaurant is a good setting for the culinary creations of master-chef Michael Caines. The set-price lunches are particularly good value. ⊗ *Map P2 • Cathedral Yard, Exeter • 01392 223638 • Closed Sun • £££££*

5 Steamers
Tucked in behind an art gallery, Steamers offers fresh fish with a Mediterranean twist. The two-course meals are a bargain. ⊗ *Map M4 • New Cut, Beer • 01297 22922 • Closed Mon & Sun dinner • £££*

6 Rockfish Seafood & Chips
Mitch Tonk's seafood restaurant is set in laid-back yet chic surroundings. Try the gourmet fish and chips and ice-cream sundaes. ⊗ *Map K6 • 8 South Embankment, Dartmouth • 01803 832800 • Open noon–9:30pm Mon–Sun (summer) • ££*

7 22 Mill Street
Hidden away in a tranquil Dartmoor village, 22 Mill Street has an upmarket feel and a modern European menu. ⊗ *Map J4 • 22 Mill St, Chagford • 01647 432244 • Closed Wed–Sun • £££££*

8 Barbican Kitchen
Set in an historic Barbican building, this relaxed brasserie attracts shoppers at lunchtime and romantic couples in the evening. ⊗ *Map Q6 • 58 Southside St, Plymouth • 01752 604448 • £££*

9 Tanners
Fine food and wine can be enjoyed in one of Plymouth's oldest buildings. The set-price menus at Tanners feature poultry, game and fresh seafood. ⊗ *Map P5 • Prysten House, Finewell St, Plymouth • 01752 252001 • Closed Sun & Mon • ££££*

10 Café Alf Resco
A local breakfast and coffee favourite, this child-friendly café with a terrace serves pastries, baguettes, and lunchtime specials. ⊗ *Map K5 • Lower Street, Dartmouth • 01803 835880 • Open 7am–2pm daily • No credit cards • £*

Unless otherwise stated, all restaurants accept credit cards and serve vegetarian meals.

Left **Tintagel Castle** Right **Newquay Zoo**

North Cornwall

WITH THE ATLANTIC HAMMERING ON THE COAST, *much of North Cornwall has a harsh feel in contrast with the more sheltered character of the county's southern seaboard. Abandoned engine houses and chimney stacks recall its industrial past, while numerous Wesleyan chapels are testament to the faith of its mining population. Between the cliffs are some of the region's best surf beaches. You can indulge in the county's finest seafood in Padstow, explore architectural styles at Prideaux Place and Lanhydrock, and enjoy the peace of the Camel Estuary. The area is rich in Arthurian connections, not least the ruins of Tintagel Castle and sites on Bodmin Moor.*

Left **The harbour at Boscastle** Right **Rick Stein's Café, Padstow**

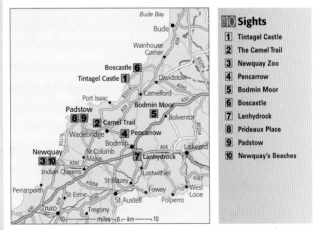

🔟 Sights

1. Tintagel Castle
2. The Camel Trail
3. Newquay Zoo
4. Pencarrow
5. Bodmin Moor
6. Boscastle
7. Lanhydrock
8. Prideaux Place
9. Padstow
10. Newquay's Beaches

www.visitnewquay.org has plenty of useful information.

1 Tintagel Castle

This coastal stronghold is one of the country's most romantic castle ruins. Its appeal is also due to its Arthurian associations, as the supposed birthplace of the Once and Future King. The structure though, probably dates from the 12th century, when it belonged to the Norman earls of Cornwall. There may already have been a Roman fortification and traces of a Celtic monastery have been found. Whatever the story, it is highly atmospheric and on a dramatic site. ◈ *Map D2*
• *Tintagel • 01840 770328 • Open Apr–Sep: 10am–6pm; Oct: 10am–5pm; Nov–Mar: 10am–4pm Sat & Sun • Adm*
• *www.english-heritage.org.uk*

2 The Camel Trail

This walking and cycling route runs for 27 km (17 miles) between Padstow and the edge of Bodmin Moor. The Padstow–Wadebridge section is on a resurfaced railway track and offers glimpses of the abundant birdlife along the Camel Estuary. From Wadebridge, the route heads southeast towards Bodmin before following the winding river through tranquil woods north to Poley's Bridge. Tourist offices at Padstow, Wadebridge and Bodmin have leaflets, detailed guides and maps. ◈ *Map D3*

3 Newquay Zoo

More than 130 species are held in such enclosures as the Tropical House, Penguin Pool, Monkey Walk, African Savanna and Wildlife at Night. The zoo has an active conservation and education agenda. Visitors can meet the animals, watch them being fed and get lost in the Dragon Maze. Look out for the graceful Red Pandas and comical lemurs, and enjoy feeding fish to the penguins and mealy worms to the meerkats. ◈ *Map C4*
• *Trenance Gardens, Newquay • 08444 742244 • Open 10am–5pm daily • Adm*
• *www.newquayzoo.org.uk*

4 Pencarrow

Inhabited by a branch of one of Cornwall's most powerful old families, this elegant Georgian house was constructed in the 1760s and stands proudly at the end of a mile-long drive. The interior boasts an arched inner hall filled with dolls and push-chairs, a music room with an exquisite Rococo ceiling and paintings by Reynolds. Outside are extensive formal and wooded gardens, designed in the 19th century by the Radical politician Sir William Molesworth.
◈ *Map D3 • Bodmin • 01208 841369*
• *Apr–Sep: 11am–5pm Sun–Thu • Adm*
• *www.pencarrow.co.uk*

Pencarrow House

Cornwall's Mineworks

An iconic image of the Cornish landscape is the engine house and chimney that denotes the existence of a former mine. North Cornwall is dotted with these castle-like granite structures. They hark back to a time when the county was producing up to two-thirds of the world's total output of copper and tin. The industry fell into decline in the 1870s.

Bodmin Moor

Cornwall's great inland wilderness is made of the same granite mass as Dartmoor and has the same mixture of rugged grandeur interspersed with splashing rivers and shady woodland. Dotted with mysterious prehistoric remains such as the Hurlers and Trethevy Quoit, the moor has a plethora of places associated with King Arthur and his knights. In the midst of the desolate expanses lie appealing villages, such as Blisland, St Neot's and Altarnun. ⊗ *Map E3*

Boscastle

The great wall of cliffs making up much of North Cornwall's coast is sliced through by the Valency and Jordan rivers here, which twist through a ravine to a tiny harbour. The village was devastated by a flash flood in 2004, but the damage has been repaired and Boscastle has reverted to its natural serenity. Look out for the famous blowhole known as Devil's Bellows, below Penally Point. ⊗ *Map D2*

Lanhydrock

The finest house in Cornwall is a must-see. Originally Jacobean, little of the original construction survived a fire in 1881, but the Victorian interior visible today – lovingly restored by the National Trust – makes up for the loss. The 50-odd rooms include the rather cramped maids' bedrooms and the lavish quarters of the Agar-Robartes family, but the highlights are the impressive kitchens and sculleries. The huge gardens and wooded parkland are wonderful and worth exploring *(see pp8–9).*

Prideaux Place

This historic mansion blends Elizabethan splendour with 18th-century Gothic decor. Highlights include the Great Chamber, with biblical tales illustrated on the plaster ceiling, and the oak-panelled Great Hall, now a dining room, showing a frieze of small animals. Look out for the carving of Elizabeth I

Golitha Falls on the Fowey River, Bodmin Moor

Prideaux Place

standing on a pig (a symbol of vice) next to the fireplace. The morning room has paintings by the Cornish portrait artist John Opie *(see p30)*.

Padstow

Both fishing port and seaside resort, Padstow has also developed a significant profile as Cornwall's gastronomic capital. Ever since seafood champion Rick Stein established a restaurant here in the 1970s, the town has become synonymous with gourmet food. The premier beaches nearby attract both surfers and families. The May Day Obby Oss festivities are among the country's most theatrical and the sheltered Camel Estuary boasts great walking and cycling routes *(see pp30–31)*.

Newquay's Beaches

After the arrival of the railway in the 1870s, Newquay developed as a beach resort. It is now one of Britain's pre-eminent surf resorts, hosting numerous competitions at Fistral Beach. Holywell Bay and Perran Beach are also highly regarded, while the more sheltered Towan Beach, Tolcarne and Lusty Glaze are suitable for families. Watergate Bay attracts the extreme sports crowd. ⊗ *Map C4*

A Drive Along Cornwall's Northern Coast

Morning

Cornwall's northernmost resort of **Bude** has fine beaches for a morning dip. From here, the A39 plunges south; branch off onto the B3263 to **Boscastle** for a stroll along its harbour, which has a **Museum of Witchcraft**. On the way in or out of the village, stop at St Juliot's church, where Thomas Hardy once worked as an architect. Six km (4 miles) west is **Tintagel** *(see p83)*, one of Cornwall's popular sights on account of its ruined castle said to have been Arthur's birthplace. After touring the castle, lunch in a local café, or escape the crowds by heading south to the harbour village of **Port Isaac** *(see p86)*.

Afternoon

After lunch, head inland to **Bodmin**, an ancient market town featuring Cornwall's largest parish church. You can also visit the **Bodmin Jail** *(see p86)* and the Courtroom Experience next to the tourist office, where you can cast your vote in a re-enactment of a celebrated murder trial of 1844. From **Bodmin**, take the A30 west to **Newquay**, which has some of Cornwall's best beaches. The county's only zoo is located here. Head up the coast on the B3276 and stop at **Watergate Bay** *(see p41)*, where the **Beach Hut** *(see p87)* is a great spot for snacks. Surfing equipment can be hired from the **Extreme Academy**. Continue up the B3276 to **Padstow** and dine at one of its seafood restaurants.

Discover more at www.bodminlive.com, www.bodminmoor.co.uk and www.visitboscastleandtintagel.com.

85

Left **Port Isaac** Right **Cardinham Woods**

Best of the Rest

1 Trerice
This Elizabethan National Trust manor has a splendid barrel-roofed Great Chamber. You can play kayles (Cornish skittles) in the grounds. ◈ *Map C4 • Kestle Mill, Newquay • 01637 875404 • Open mid-Feb–Oct: 11am–5pm daily • Adm*

2 Port Isaac
A typical North Cornish fishing village with winding lanes and a working harbour. The surrounding cliffs offer fine walking. ◈ *Map D3*

3 Tintagel Old Post Office
This 14th-century manor house is furnished with local oak pieces. ◈ *Map D3 • Fore St, Tintagel • 01840 770024 • Open Apr–Sep 10:30am– 5:30pm daily; Oct 11am–4pm daily • Adm*

4 Bedruthan Steps
The jagged slate outcrops on this beach were supposed to be the stepping stones of the giant Bedruthan. A cliffside staircase descends to the beach but bathing is unsafe. ◈ *Map C3*

5 Cardinham Woods
There are four forest walks and a waymarked trail for mountain-bikers in these woods. ◈ *Map E3 • Bikes available for hire*

6 Blue Reef Aquarium
Get close to everything from sea horses to octopuses in this aquarium near Newquay harbour. ◈ *Map C4 • Towan Promenade, Newquay • 01637 878134 • 10am–4pm daily; summer: closes 5pm • Adm*

7 Bodmin Jail
Built in 1779, this former jail is a fascinating attraction, with tours of the cells, visits to the "execution pit" and a ghost walk offered to visitors. ◈ *Map D4*
• Berrycombe Rd, Bodmin • 01208 76292
• Open 9:30am–5pm daily • Adm
• www.bodminjail.org

8 St Enodoc
This tiny 13th-century church appears hidden amid dunes in the middle of a golf course. Poet John Betjeman is buried here.
◈ *Map D3 • Daymer Bay • 01208 863178*

9 Crackington Haven
This highly scenic beach is backed by dramatic cliffs rising to 130 m (430 ft), with strangely contorted rock strata. ◈ *Map E2*

10 East Pool Mine
Two great beam engines are preserved in their engine houses at this museum. ◈ *Map C5 • Pool, Redruth • 01209 315027 • Open mid-Mar–Oct 10:30am–5pm Tue–Sat • Adm*

Price Categories

For a three-course	£	under £20
meal for one with	££	£20–£35
half a bottle of wine,	£££	£35–£45
including taxes and	££££	£45–£55
extra charges.	£££££	over £55

Rick Stein's flagship Seafood Restaurant

Places to Eat

1 The Seafood Restaurant
The flagship of Rick Stein's culinary empire offers a range of fish dishes from cod, chips and peas to Indonesian seafood curry and lobster. Booking is essential. 🅂 *Map D3 • Riverside, Padstow • 01841 532700 • £££££*

2 St Petroc's Bistro
Smaller than The Seafood Restaurant, this Stein venture has fewer choices on the menu and lower prices, but delivers the goods. Meat gets equal billing with seafood. 🅂 *Map D3 • 4 New St, Padstow • 01841 532700 • £££*

3 Paul Ainsworth at No.6
Dress up for dining in this Georgian town house with contemporary decor and sophisticated food. 🅂 *Map D3 • 6 Middle St, Padstow • 01841 532093 • £££££*

4 Fifteen
A bevy of young chefs show their culinary expertise in Jamie Oliver's restaurant in a fantastic location overlooking the beach. The food has a strong Italian stamp. 🅂 *Map C4 • Watergate Bay • 01637 861000 • £££££*

5 Nathan Outlaw
Awarded two Michelin Stars, Cornwall's foremost fine dining restaurant offers a daily changing six-course tasting menu, featuring the freshest seafood. Vegetarian menu served on request. 🅂 *Map D3 • St Enodoc Hotel, Rock • 01208 862737 • £££££*

6 Stein's Fish & Chips
The most affordable and relaxed of Stein's eateries, this place has some of the most succulent fish and chips in the West Country. 🅂 *Map D3 • South Quay, Padstow • 01841 532700 • £*

7 Lewinnick Lodge
Choose to eat at the terrace, restaurant, beer garden or bar, to relish the seafood specialities on the daily changing menu. Enjoy the coastal views as you dine. 🅂 *Map C4 • Pentire Headland, Newquay • 01637 878117 • £££*

8 Life's a Beach
This restaurant is located right on the beach. By day, it serves baguettes, burgers and ice cream, and transforms into a fancy restaurant serving British and European dishes in the evening. 🅂 *Map E2 • Summerleaze Beach, Bude • 01288 355222 • £££*

9 No.1 Rock Road
This modern bistro affords good views across the Camel Estuary and Padstow. It serves dishes such as crab sandwiches, Cornish lamb and local Porthilly mussels. 🅂 *Map D3 • Beachside, Rock • 01208 863008 • £££*

10 The Beach Hut
With the same stunning beachside location as Fifteen, this is a casual place for evening meals in summer. Fish specials and burgers are on the menu. 🅂 *Map C4 • Watergate Bay • 01637 860877 • £££*

Left **A boatyard on the River Fal, Roseland Peninsula** Right **Royal Cornwall Museum**

South Cornwall

WITH ITS INDENTED COASTLINE AND NUMEROUS RIVER ESTUARIES interspersed with secluded settlements, this is a region of unexpected surprises. The charms of Fowey and fishing villages such as Polperro and Mevagissey should not be missed. Cornwall's capital, Truro, is small enough to negotiate easily on foot. Its cathedral and the Royal Cornwall Museum are the main sights. The most famous attraction however, is the Eden Project, a high-tech garden for the third millennium. South Cornwall's other major gardens, Trelissick and Heligan, are must-sees for plant fans, while south of here, the picturesque Roseland Peninsula is good for exploring.

Sights

1. Eden Project
2. Lost Gardens of Heligan
3. Roseland Peninsula
4. Royal Cornwall Museum
5. Polperro
6. St Mawes Castle
7. Fowey
8. Truro Cathedral
9. Trelissick Garden
10. Cotehele House

A view of the River Fowey from Saints' Way

Preceding pages **St Michael's Mount**

Eden Project

Eden Project

Since opening in a former clay pit in 2001, this has become one of Cornwall's success stories. With its giant greenhouses and imaginative scope, Eden is much more than just an upmarket theme park. Rather, it describes itself as a "living theatre of plants and people" – a fantastic illustration of the diversity of the Earth's plant life. Above all, the striking beauty of these plants make this an essential stop and one worth visiting at different times of the year in order to capture its seasonal changes *(see pp10–11)*.

Lost Gardens of Heligan

"Lost" for 70 years and neglected for even longer, this salvaged Victorian garden is a triumph of horticultural skill. Presenting a splendid pageantry of plants in diverse habitats including ferneries, fruit houses, Italian gardens and a productive Kitchen Garden, this subtropical "Jungle" and "Lost Valley" will appeal to both adults and kids. There is a strong emphasis on conservation and indoor plasma screens allow visitors to observe the wildlife at close quarters. *Map D4 • Pentewan, St Austell • 01726 845100 • Open Apr–Sep: 10am–6pm daily; Oct–Mar: 10am–5pm daily • Adm • www.heligan.com*

Roseland Peninsula

A sleepy backwater planted with lush palms and subtropical vegetation, Roseland Peninsula is edged by low cliffs with fine sea views from St Anthony's Head. There are idyllic creeks and sheltered beaches to explore, as well as sailing boats and kayaks to hire. The secluded churches of St Just-in-Roseland and St Anthony-in-Roseland are also worth viewing. The peninsula can be comfortably toured by bicycle, and may be reached via the year-round Falmouth– St Mawes passenger ferry. From St Mawes, a summer ferry crosses to Place, not far from St Anthony Head. *Map C5*

Royal Cornwall Museum

This museum is a cornucopia of Cornish culture, embracing everything from Bronze Age pottery to Newlyn art. The minerals display, based on a collection made 200 years ago, is of international significance. You can also admire the impressive collection of fossils. Botanical and zoological specimens are beautifully represented by items as diverse as stuffed puffins, butterflies, shells and pressed plants. Regular and varied exhibitions are held here. *Map C5 • River Street, Truro • 01872 272205 • Open 10am–4:45pm Mon–Sat*

Lost Gardens of Heligan

The China Clay Story

No one passing through the St Austell area can fail to notice the vast conical spoil heaps linked to the local china clay industry. The substance is used in a variety of products, from paint and paper to medicines. You can learn about its history and applications at the fascinating Wheal Martyn (see p94).

The fishing village of Polperro

Polperro

At peak times, this classic Cornish fishing village gets rather too commercialized and crowded, but visit out of season, or step out early in the morning, and you can appreciate its authentic charm. A long main street, mostly traffic-free, leads down alongside a stream and quaint cottages to a huddle of houses around the harbour. An old pilchard factory holds an absorbing smuggling and fishing museum. Good coastal walks begin from here. ✆ Map E4

St Mawes Castle

Though the lesser of the two 16th-century artillery forts at the mouth of the Carrick Roads Estuary (the other is Pendennis), this castle is better preserved and sports heraldic devices and Latin inscriptions dedicated to Henry VIII and Edward VI. The interior has living quarters and gun rooms displaying ships' cannons from the 1800s, and an impressive bronze "saker" cannon of about 1560, cast by Venetian gunmaster Alberghetti and recovered from the sea off the Devon coast.
✆ Map C5 • St Mawes • 01326 270526 • Open Apr–Sep: 10am–6pm daily; Oct: closes 5pm; Nov–Feb: 10am–4pm Sat & Sun • Adm • www.english-heritage.org.uk

Fowey

Climbing up the west bank of the River Fowey, this was one of the foremost ports of medieval England and is still a busy harbour town. Most of the maritime activity, however, is now to do with pleasure boats anchored in the estuary. It is worth hiring a boat to enjoy the beauty of the river. ✆ Map E4

Truro Cathedral

Cornwall's capital is over-shadowed by the soaring spires of its cathedral, a Neo-Gothic confection completed in 1910. The faux-medieval style is the cause of much debate in this predominantly Georgian city, but there is no denying the impact of its impressive interior. The Robartes Memorial, showing effigies of a merchant and his wife propped on their elbows, is one of the eye-catching monuments within. Free guided tours are offered in summer. ✆ Map C5 • St Mary's St, Truro • 01872 276782

St Mawes Castle

The St Mawes passenger ferry connects the castle with Falmouth See p98.

Trelissick Garden

This lovely, extensive garden has lawns, flowerbeds and hollows filled with rare plants and shrubs, sprawling parkland and miles of woodland paths with panoramic views of the River Fal. Late April, early May and September are the best times to visit, though there is always something to see. A gallery shows Cornish craftwork.
◈ Map C5 • Feock • 01872 862090
• Open mid-Feb–Oct: 10:30am–5:30pm daily; Nov–mid-Feb: 11am–4pm • Adm

Cotehele House

The excellent condition of this Tudor abode is due to its abandonment by its owners, the Edgcumbe family, who left it intact for a more accessible home outside Plymouth (see pp14–15). It remained with the family until the National Trust took over in 1947. The house has original furniture, armour and a collection of embroideries and tapestries, best seen on a bright day as the rooms have no electric light. ◈ Map F3 • St Dominick, Saltash • 01579 351346 • Open mid-Mar–Oct: 11am– 4pm Sat-Thu • Adm

Truro Cathedral

A Driving Tour in South Cornwall

Morning

Start your journey in **Looe**, a traditional resort that has gained a reputation as a shark-fishing centre. A 6-km (4-mile) drive from here takes you to **Polperro**, whose tightly packed houses and minuscule harbour are best appreciated before the crowds arrive. There is a small smuggling and fishing museum here. From Polperro, a scenic minor road leads west to Bodinnick village, where regular ferries cross to **Fowey**. It has a good selection of pubs and bistros that would make suitable lunch stops (there is a car park near the ferry quay). Before or after eating, take a stroll around **Fowey**, to see **St Catherine's Castle**, one of Henry VIII's fortifications, or follow the **Hall Walk** (see p36).

Afternoon

From **Fowey**, take the A3082 to **St Austell**, from which the A390, B3287 and A3078 will bring you to **St Mawes** on the Carrick Roads Estuary. Here, a large Henrician castle offers views over the river. If you have time, explore the **Roseland Peninsula** (see p91), an area of backwaters and churches. North of St Mawes, **Trelissick Garden** offers captivating woodland walks. The King Harry ferry crosses the river, from where it is a short drive to the county capital, **Truro**. Dominated by its Neo-Gothic cathedral and an excellent museum, this relaxed city has a good choice of restaurants and accommodation.

Check out www.visit-southeastcornwall.co.uk, www.stmawesand theroseland.co.uk, www.fowey.co.uk and www.visittruro.org.uk.

93

Left **Titanic display at the Shipwreck and Heritage Centre** Right **The ruins of Restormel Castle**

TOP 10 Best of the Rest

1 Shipwreck and Heritage Centre

This collection holds discoveries from over 150 shipwrecks, including memorabilia from the *Titanic* – both the film and the wreck. ◎ *Map D4 • Quay Rd, Charlestown • 01726 69897 • Open Mar–Oct: 10am–5pm daily • Adm • www.shipwreckcharlestown.com*

2 Restormel Castle

This excellent example of a circular shell keep dates from the 13th century. The parapet offers marvellous views over the Fowey Valley. ◎ *Map E4 • Lostwithiel • 01208 872687 • Open Apr–Oct • Adm • www.english-heritage.org.uk*

3 Veryan

Close to good beaches, Veryan is known for its 200-year-old circular houses designed to prevent the devil from hiding in corners. ◎ *Map D5*

4 Mount Edgcumbe

Rebuilt after World War II, this 16th-century house has fine displays of Chinese porcelain and Flemish tapestries *(see p14)*.

5 Carrick Roads Estuary

This estuary complex is one of the world's largest natural harbours. It has lovely coastal walks and sandy coves. ◎ *Map C5*

6 Mevagissey

With its long tradition of fishing and smuggling, this busy port is worth visiting for its museum, pubs and seafood. ◎ *Map D5*

7 King Harry Ferry

Vehicles travelling between St Mawes and Falmouth can save several miles by taking this chain-driven ferry across the Fal, in operation here since 1888. ◎ *Map C5 • Feock, Truro • 01872 863132 • www.falriver.co.uk*

8 Caerhays Castle

Take a guided tour of this 19th-century castle, which forms an elegant backdrop to Porthluney Cove beach. ◎ *Map D5 • Gorran, St Austell • 01872 501310 • Open mid-Mar–mid-June: tours 11am–3pm Mon–Fri • Adm • www.caerhays.co.uk*

9 Wheal Martyn

This place provides a fascinating insight into the china clay industry, with interactive displays projecting local history. Nature trails are also organized here. ◎ *Map D4 • Wheal Martyn, St Austell • 01726 850362 • Times vary • Adm • www.wheal-martyn.com*

10 Castle Dore

This Iron Age hillfort, with concentric rings of defensive ridges, is considered the palace of the legendary King Mark of Cornwall. ◎ *Map E4 • Golant*

For more on Mevagissey, go to www.mevagissey-cornwall.co.uk.

Price Categories

For a three-course meal for one with half a bottle of wine, including taxes and extra charges.

£	under £20
££	£20–£35
£££	£35–£45
££££	£45–£55
£££££	over £55

The terrace at Hotel Tresanton

10 Places to Eat

Bustophers
This long-standing Truro bistro boasts contemporary decor, a keen local sourcing policy and flexible dining options all day long: lunch, afternoon tea and an intricate evening menu. ◈ Map C5 • 62 Lemon St, Truro • 01872 279029 • £££

Sam's
A buzzy place with a rock 'n' roll feel. The menu here includes salads, burgers, grills and fish *bouillabaisse*. Queues form at busy times (no reservations). ◈ Map E4 • 20 Fore St, Fowey • 01726 832273 • ££

Driftwood Restaurant
Fresh seafood and local meat dishes are the mainstays of the menu at this elegant hotel-restaurant perched above the sea, offering fine views. ◈ Map C5 • Rosevine, Portscatho • 01872 580644 • Open only for dinner daily • £££££

Eden Project
Local, seasonal ingredients are used at the restaurants at the Eden site, offering vegetarian, vegan and gluten-free options *(see p11)*.

Looe Brasserie
Housed in the attractive Barclay House hotel, this elegant restaurant offers fish from Looe Bay and mussels from the River Fowey. Round off the meal with Cornish cheeses. ◈ Map E4 • St Martins Rd, East Looe • 01503 262929 • Closed Sun & Mon • £££

The Kitchen
This simple, intimate restaurant serves up excellent fish and meat dishes, clotted cream desserts and Cornish cheeses. ◈ Map E4 • The Coombes, Polpero • 01503 272780 • Open Tue–Sat, closed Jan–mid-Feb • £££

Saffron
This friendly bistro offers grilled seafood, meat and eclectic wines. Saturday brunches and early-evening menus are good value. ◈ Map C5 • 5 Quay St, Truro • 01872 263771 • Closed Sun • £££

Hotel Tresanton
Modern Mediterranean food is served in this hotel overlooking the sea. A terrace offers alfresco dining. ◈ Map C5 • 27 Lower Castle Rd, St Mawes • 01326 270055 • ££££

Q
This restaurant at the Old Quay House Hotel *(see p116)*, enjoys splendid views over the River Fowey and immaculate food to match. ◈ Map E4 • Old Quay House Hotel, 28 Fore St, Fowey • 01726 833302 • Apr–May no lunch Tue; times vary in winter • £££

Dwelling House
The tiers of scrumptious cakes and delectable scones on view in the window of this period tea room lure visitors inside. There's a menu of leaf teas to go with the chosen treat. ◈ Map E4 • 6 Fore St, Fowey • 01726 833662 • £

Left **Cliffs at Land's End** Right **Penlee House in Penzance**

West Cornwall and the Isles of Scilly

FOR MANY, THE WESTERN END OF CORNWALL – and of Britain – is the quintessence of everything that makes the county special. Here, you will find every kind of landscape and settlement that Cornwall has to offer, from the sailing port of Falmouth to the fishing hamlet of Mousehole, from the bare moorland of the Penwith Peninsula to the sandy Whitesand Bay, and from the creeks of the River Helford to the inhospitable cliffs at Zennor. Poke around the region's numerous prehistoric remains and explore the island stronghold of St Michael's Mount. The great headlands of Land's End and Lizard Point bring you face-to-face with the raging Atlantic Ocean, but you can get closer still by venturing out to the beautiful Isles of Scilly.

St Michael's Mount

🔟 Sights

1. Tresco Abbey Gardens
2. Pendennis Castle
3. Barbara Hepworth Museum and Sculpture Garden
4. St Michael's Mount
5. Tate St Ives
6. Minack Theatre
7. St Ives
8. Isles of Scilly
9. Penzance
10. Land's End

1 Tresco Abbey Gardens

This subtropical oasis on the Isles of Scilly was created in 1834 and nurtured by five generations of the same family. Tresco's unique microclimate and the establishment of tall windbreaks have allowed the gardens to thrive. Currently, over 20,000 plants representing around 200 species from places as diverse as Chile, South Africa and Australia are reared here. Remnants from the ruined priory and modern sculptures create the perfect setting, and there is an interesting collection of ships' figureheads taken from local wrecks (see pp22–3).

2 Pendennis Castle

Fortified by Henry VIII in the 1540s, this formidable castle guarding the Carrick Roads Estuary endured a 5-month siege during the English Civil War before falling to Parliamentarian forces. Its stout walls hold the governor's residence, a Tudor fortress in the central keep, and Edwardian and Victorian barracks. Kids will enjoy going down the tunnels to the big guns and magazine in Half Moon Battery. The views from here are terrific. Guided tours are available. ⊗ Map C5 • Falmouth • 01326 316594 • Open Apr–Sep: 10am–6pm daily; Oct: 10am–5pm daily; Nov–Mar: 10am–4pm Sat & Sun • Adm • www.english-heritage.org.uk

Pendennis Castle

Barbara Hepworth Sculpture Garden

3 Barbara Hepworth Museum and Sculpture Garden

One of the foremost sculptors of the 20th century, Hepworth was inspired by the granite landscape of West Cornwall and settled in St Ives in 1939. Her sleek, abstract sculptures can be seen in her former studio located in the heart of St Ives. The smaller works are displayed inside, but the true glory of the place is the adjoining walled, thickly planted garden – an ideal setting for her large-scale geometric forms (see p27).

4 St Michael's Mount

The dominant feature in Mount's Bay, this castle residence lies a short way out to sea and can be reached by causeway or passenger ferry. The drama of arrival does not end there, for visitors must make a steep climb to reach the house itself. Most impressive among the cosy warren of rooms within are the Tudor Great Hall, with its hunting frieze and the dainty Blue Drawing Room. Other rooms hold armour, weaponry and mementos. The views from the battlements are stupendous (see pp28–9).

There is a concession for joint visits to the Hepworth and Tate museums.

Boat Trips from Falmouth

Ferries leave for St Mawes from Falmouth's Prince of Wales Pier, all year (1–2 hourly; 20 min). In summer, you can also board boats to Trelissick, Truro (up to 5pm daily) and the hamlet of Flushing on the River Penryn (1–2 hourly), or explore the River Fal and other local estuaries on self-drive cabin cruisers. Check details on www.falriver.co.uk.

Tate St Ives

A beacon of modern art, this gallery pays homage to the local schools of art that flourished in the area, while also showcasing contemporary works, usually with a local connection. Converted from a gasworks in 1993, the building is a modernist statement by itself and is located just across from Porthminster beach. Natural light floods the white-walled rooms, providing an ideal background for the abstract and avant-garde works on display. The rooftop terrace offers stunning ocean views. The gallery closes for several days three to four times a year for hanging, so call before visiting (see p26).

Tate St Ives

Minack Theatre

The vision of one woman, Rowena Cade (see p25), the Minack is a unique attraction in Cornwall. Just like a Roman amphitheatre on some Mediterranean shore, the theatre has been carved out of the cliff-face above the sea, creating a magical setting for watching plays and musicals. Shows are performed from April through to September, though the Exhibition Centre is open all year. Contrary to what you might expect, cancellations due to bad weather are rare, but it's advisable to wrap up warmly (see pp24–5).

St Ives

There is a distinctly Mediterranean flavour about this seaside town with its maze of flowery lanes climbing up the hill. This, combined with the clear light and rugged landscape, was a major draw for the succession of artists who settled here, renting studios from local fishermen. Today, tourists have replaced pilchards as the town's mainstay, thronging its sandy beaches, numerous galleries and elegant restaurants every summer. If you wish to escape the crowds, climb up to The Island, a grassy headland with lofty views across St Ives Bay (see pp26–7).

Isles of Scilly

It takes an effort to reach the Isles of Scilly, but few come away disappointed. Imagined by some to be the remains of the lost land of Lyonnesse, the scattered archipelago is breathtakingly beautiful, presenting inspiring vistas in every direction. The beaches here are among the best in the country, but when the sea is up,

Find more information at www.westcornwall.org.uk, www.stivestic.co.uk and www.visitislesofscilly.com.

The Minack amphitheatre

the best place to be is in Hell Bay, Bryher, to experience the full fury of an Atlantic storm. ◈ Map A4

9 Penzance

Draped over a hill above a harbour, Penzance has plenty of charm and possesses two of Cornwall's best museum-galleries: Penlee House and The Exchange. All the glories of the Penwith Peninsula are easily accessible from this pleasant town, from the abbey-fortress of St Michael's Mount to the coves and beaches of the rocky coast. For historical character, look no further than the handsome buildings of Chapel Street, including Egyptian House, and Market Jew Street, with Market House at the top *(see pp28–9)*.

10 Land's End

The western tip of the British mainland has an age-old fascination and offers fine coastal sights. The headland offers panoramic views over the undulating coast and to rocky outcrops out at sea with such intriguing names as the Armed Knight, the Irish Lady and Dr Syntax Head. The Longships lighthouse, 2 km (1.5 miles) out, is also usually visible. Sometimes you can also spot the Wolf Rock lighthouse, 15 km (9 miles) to the southwest and even the Isles of Scilly, 45 km (28 miles) away. ◈ Map A6

A Walk from Newlyn to Porthcurno

Morning

🕐 If you're in **Newlyn** early enough, look in on the fish auction that takes place here every morning. Start your walk along a cycle-path running south from the harbour. After about 2 km (1 mile), you will reach the bijou fishing village of **Mousehole** (pronounced "Mowzul"). The place was ransacked by a Spanish raiding party in 1595, who reputedly left just one building standing – the 14th-century **Keigwin House,** which is still standing. Walk through the village and pick up the coast path heading south. You reach **Point Spaniard** where the raiders suppo-sedly landed. The path then swerves inland before meeting the coast again at **Carn Du,** the eastern point of **Lamorna Cove.** Stop for lunch at the **Lamorna Wink** pub.

Afternoon

From Lamorna the path sticks close to the rocky coast. Follow it past **Tater Du** lighthouse and round Boscawen Point to **St Loy's Cove.** For this stretch of the walk there are no cafés, so make sure you stock up with snacks. After a short walk, mainly on the clifftop, you will reach unspoiled **Penberth Cove** – little more than a few cottages and fishing boats. Conti-nue along the clifftop, past the Iron Age fort of **Treryn Dinas** *(see p25),* where you can see the famous **Logan Rock.** From here the path descends to **Porthcurno,** which has a café and pub, a museum of telegraphy and the **Minack Theatre.**

Around Devon and Cornwall – West Cornwall and the Isles of Scilly

Left **Grey seal at the National Seal Sanctuary** Right **Boat displayed at the Maritime Museum**

Best of the Rest

1 National Seal Sanctuary
Sick or injured seals are brought to this sanctuary from all over the country. Tour the pools and a specially designed hospital, and view ponies and otters.
◈ Map B5 • Gweek, Helston • 01326 221361 • Open Apr–Oct: 10am–5pm daily; Nov–Apr: 10am–4pm daily • Adm

2 National Maritime Museum, Cornwall
This museum in a former boatyard holds a riveting variety of vessels and nautical equipment. ◈ Map C5 • Discovery Quay, Falmouth • 01326 313388 • Open 10am–5pm daily • Adm

3 Falmouth Art Gallery
A fine collection of work by Victorian painters and British Impressionists is on display here. Children's book illustrations and maritime art are also featured.
◈ Map C5 • The Moor, Falmouth • 01326 313863 • Open 10am–5pm Mon–Sat

4 Tremenheere Sculpture Gardens
Contemporary sculpture and art installations, blended with lush subtropical planting in a sheltered valley. ◈ Map B5 • Gulval, Penzance • 01736 448089 • Times vary • Adm

5 Geevor Tin Mine
Tour the surface works and the 18th-century tunnels at the UK's largest preserved mining site. ◈ Map A5 • Trewellard, Pendeen, St Just • 01736 788662 • Open Apr–Oct: 9am–5pm Sun–Fri; Nov–Mar: 9am–4pm Sun–Fri • Adm

6 Wayside Museum and Trewey Mill
Discover a hotch-potch of over 5,000 items relating to Cornwall.
◈ Map A5 • Zennor • 01736 796945 • Open May–Sep: 10:30am–5:30pm daily; Apr & Oct: 10:30am–4:30pm daily • Adm

7 Western Rocks, Isles of Scilly
Boat tours can be taken around these rocks on the fringes of the archipelago. ◈ Map A4

8 Lizard Lighthouse
This lighthouse on the mainland's most southerly point was erected in 1752, and has distinctive twin towers. ◈ Map C6 • Lizard Point • 01326 290202 • Times vary • Adm

9 Isles of Scilly Museum
Local shipwrecks have contributed many of the exhibits in this museum, which include stuffed birds and art. ◈ Map B4 • Church Street, St Mary's • 01720 422337 • Open Apr–Sep: 10am–4:30pm Mon–Fri, till 2pm Sat; Oct–Mar: 10am–2pm Mon–Sat • Adm

10 River Helford
Hire a boat to explore this complex of inlets and shady creeks. Tea rooms along the way provide refreshments. ◈ Map C5

The National Seal Sanctuary offers a good discount on tickets bought online.

Left **Lanyon Quoit** Right **Men-an-Tol on moorland near Penzance**

Prehistoric Sites in West Cornwall

Chun Castle
The walls of this Iron Age hillfort are mainly collapsed, but in parts reach a height of 3 m (9 ft), and the gateposts still stand. The ruined huts inside date from the Dark Ages.
Ⓢ Map A5 • Near Morvah, off B3318

Chun Quoit
On open moorland, this quoit – a neolithic chamber tomb topped by a flat stone and resembling a giant granite mushroom – dates from around 2,000 BC.
Ⓢ Map A5 • Near Morvah, off B3318

Chysauster
Cornwall's most complete prehistoric monument consists of stone-walled houses arranged around courtyards, where you can discern hearths, basins and drains. Ⓢ Map A5 • Near Zennor
• 07831 757934 • Times vary • Adm

Men-an-Tol
The Cornish name (meaning stone-with-a-hole) accurately describes this Bronze Age monument that was long thought to have healing powers. Situated on moorland, it is 2,500–4,000 years old. Ⓢ Map A5
• Near Morvah, off Morvah–Madron Road

Lanyon Quoit
Also known as the Giant's Quoit or Giant's Table, this capped burial chamber is one of the most accessible of West Penwith's prehistoric remains.
Ⓢ Map A5 • Near Morvah

Tregiffian Burial Chamber
This barrow tomb revealed an urn and cremated bones when it was excavated in 1967.
Ⓢ Map A6 • Near Lamorna, off B3315

The Merry Maidens
Considered Cornwall's most perfect stone circle. Legend has it, that it is the remains of 19 maidens turned to stone for carousing on the Sabbath.
Ⓢ Map A6 • Near Lamorna, off B3315

Halliggye Fougou
This is one of the most impressive of West Cornwall's *fogous* – long, underground structures from the Iron Age.
Ⓢ Map C6 • Trelowarren, Mawgan, Helston • 01326 221224 • Open Apr–Oct

Bant's Carn, Isles of Scilly
One of the Isles' many megalithic monuments, this burial chamber on St Mary's has a roof made of four huge slabs.
Ⓢ Map B4 • Halangy Down, St Mary's

Porth Hellick Barrow, Isles of Scilly
In the southeastern corner of St Mary's, this is the best preserved tomb in the Scillies.
Ⓢ Map B4 • Porth Hellick Down, St Mary's

Left **Ship Inn** Centre **Tinners Arms** Right **Porthmeor Beach Café**

Cafés and Pubs

Porthgwidden Café
Right above the beach, yet in St Ives' centre, this summer café is ideal for a restorative snack after exposure to sun and sea. ◈ *Map B5 • Porthgwidden Beach, St Ives • 01736 796791*

Gylly Beach Café
A great location on Falmouth's main beach makes this a perfect stop for sandwiches, salads and cold drinks. ◈ *Map C5 • Cliff Rd, Falmouth • 01326 312884*

Victoria Inn
This pink-painted pub has a cosy bar and a popular restaurant next door. It serves locally inspired mains, including fresh fish, and tempting desserts. ◈ *Map B5 • Perranuthnoe • 01736 710309*

New Inn
This classy pub serves bar snacks as well as lavish feasts. It is famous for its local Bryher lobster and grass-fed beef steak combination. ◈ *Map A4 • Tresco, Isles of Scilly • 01720 422844*

Turk's Head
Considered by island cognoscenti to be the best drinker on the Scillies, this pub is also famous for its pasties. ◈ *Map A4 • St Agnes, Isles of Scilly • 01720 422434*

Blue Anchor Inn
Enjoy the medieval atmosphere at this former monks' resthouse dating from the 15th century. Cosy nooks and home-brewed Spingo ales are the main attractions. Snacks are available. ◈ *Map B5 • 50 Coinagehall St, Helston • 01326 562821*

Peppercorn Kitchen Café
Located close to the beach, this tiny café serves creative lunches, hot drinks and a tempting selection of puddings. There are picnic tables outside and a wood burner during cold weather. ◈ *Map B5 • Lynfield Yard, Perranuthnoe • 01736 719584*

Tinners Arms
D H Lawrence was a customer during his stay in Zennor, but the place has been elegantly renovated since then, with bare floorboards and an open fire. Enjoy good ales with the hearty meals served here. ◈ *Map A5 • Zennor • 01736 796927*

Ship Inn
You can almost feel the sea spray in this fisherman's pub above the harbour, full of maritime character. Crab and fish with chunky chips are usually on the menu. ◈ *Map A5 • South Cliff, Mousehole • 01736 731234*

Porthmeor Beach Café
This chic café, located just above Porthmeor Beach, affords great views. The imaginative food is inspired by far-flung cuisines. Their dessert tapas are sublime. ◈ *Map B5 • Porthmeor, St Ives • 01736 793366*

Price Categories

For a three-course meal for one with half a bottle of wine, including taxes and extra charges.	**£** under £20
	££ £20–£35
	£££ £35–£45
	££££ £45–£55
	£££££ over £55

Porthminster Beach Café

 Restaurants

The Wheel House
This quayside shellfish café serves up simple oyster, mussel, prawn and crab dishes in *cataplanas* (Portuguese dishes), plus house wine. ❧ *Map C5 • Upton Slip, Falmouth • 01326 318050 • Open Wed–Sat for dinner • No credit cards • £*

Blas Burgerworks
St Ives' gourmet burger restaurant serves excellent chargrilled Cornish beefburgers with all the trimmings. Communal tables and friendly service ensure a lively atmosphere. ❧ *Map B5 • The Warren, St Ives • 01736 797272 • £*

2 Fore Street
Head to this relaxed French-style bistro right by the harbour for simple, zesty food such as potted Newlyn crab. Enjoy the walled garden in summer. ❧ *Map A5 • 2 Fore St, Mousehole • 01736 731164 • Closed Oct–Apr Mon & Tue • £££*

The Beach
Relax on the terrace here and gaze out over the beach while you dine. The local seafood on the menu adds to the restaurant's attractions. ❧ *Map A5 • Sennen Cove • 01736 871191 • ££*

Juliet's Garden Restaurant
A casual, modern place with outdoor tables and lovely sea views. Enjoy a daytime snack or a candle-lit dinner. ❧ *Map B4 • St Mary's, Isles of Scilly • 01720 422228 • Closed Nov–Mar • £££*

Gurnard's Head
This cheerful gastro-inn does a great fish stew among other dishes, such as crab tartlets and mackerel. Menus change according to the day's catch. ❧ *Map A5 • Zennor • 01736 796928 • £££*

Alba
A chic restaurant offering an eclectic range of dishes. Set-price menus are available at lunchtime and early evening. ❧ *Map B5 • Wharf Rd, St Ives • 01736 797222 • £££*

Kota Restaurant
This harbourside restaurant serves organic fish and farm produce. The chef, who is of Chinese, Maori and Malaysian origin, puts imaginative Asian twists on the dishes. ❧ *Map B5 • Harbour Rd, Porthleven • 01326 562407 • Closed Mon & Sun • ££££*

Hooked on the Rocks
The panoramic terrace at this beach-side eatery is a great place to enjoy a selection of tapas, lobster or crab, or Cornish *bouillabaisse*. ❧ *Map C5 • Swanpool Beach, Falmouth • 01326 311886 • £££*

Porthminster Beach Café
Beach café by day, smart and pricey restaurant at night, this place serves tasty dishes such as local mussels, scallops and monkfish curry. ❧ *Map B5 • Porthminster Beach, St Ives • 01736 795352 • Closed Mon in winter • £££*

STREETSMART

DEVON AND CORNWALL'S TOP 10

Left **Surf hire shop on Fistral Beach, Newquay** Right **A children's playground**

TOP 10 Planning Your Trip

1 What to Pack
Devon and Cornwall get more sun than any other part of Britain, but be prepared for all kinds of weather. On the coasts especially, the wind can be fierce. Walkers should pack waterproofs. Never underestimate the power of the sun – a sun hat and a good sunscreen are recommended. Chilly sea temperatures persuade many to swim in a wetsuit which, along with surf equipment and other beach gear, can be rented or bought here.

2 Currency
Most currencies can be changed for British pounds and pence at major banks and main post offices. ATMs are widely found through the region. Credit cards are accepted at most hotels, though many B&Bs will not take them. Sometimes a surcharge is added for credit card transactions.

3 Passports and Visas
Visitors from the Commonwealth and the US do not need a visa for short stays. EU citizens can stay as long as they like. Overseas visitors should check with the British embassy in their home country or their embassy in London to find out more about the visa requirements applicable to them.

4 Customs Regulations
Visitors from most EU countries can bring into the UK as much tobacco and alcohol as they can carry. Those from outside the EU face tighter restrictions but, unlike EU citizens, are entitled to a limited amount of duty-free purchases.

5 Insurance
It is advisable to take out an insurance policy that covers theft, loss of baggage and medical treatment. You can get free emergency treatment at the National Health Service, but specialist care, drugs and repatriation are costly. Keep all receipts for reimbursement. Some policies cover you for lost cash and flight cancellations, though not for injuries sustained in dangerous sports – check with your insurance company for details.

6 Driving Licence
EU citizens can use their driving licence in the UK, but should carry insurance documents and a registration certificate for any vehicle brought into the country. Other foreign nationals need an international licence.

7 Time Difference
Greenwich Mean Time (GMT) is used from late October to late March, when clocks go forward an hour for British Summer Time (BST). GMT is five hours ahead of the US Eastern Standard Time and one hour behind most European countries.

8 Electrical Appliances
The electricity supply throughout the UK is 240 volts AC. Overseas visitors will need a plug adaptor (available in the UK) for any appliances they carry. Most hotels have two-pin sockets for use by shavers only.

9 Children's Needs
Devon and Cornwall are well-supplied with children's amusements and needs. Pharmacies have a range of products for mothers and young children. Although kids are not allowed in some alcohol-serving premises, many pubs have family rooms or beer gardens where they are welcome. Some B&Bs and hotels do not permit kids under a specified age.

10 Membership Cards
Bring any membership cards for driving and heritage organizations that have reciprocal arrangements with UK bodies. English Heritage and National Trust cards allow free entry into many historical sites. An internationally recognized student card is useful for discounts on transport and sights.

Preceding pages **Diners at Fifteen restaurant**

Left **A train on the Liskeard-to-Looe line** Centre **Camel Trail** Right **King Harry Ferry**

⅐₁₀ Getting There and Around

By Plane
Regular flights connect Devon and Cornwall with many European cities. The region's main airports are in Exeter and Newquay. Land's End Airport and Newquay have year-round flights to the Isles of Scilly, while Exeter only offers flights in summer. Land's End Airport also offers scenic flights.

By Sea
Plymouth is linked by ferry with France and Spain. Between April and October, ferries cross to the Isles of Scilly from Penzance. In summer, you can reach Lundy Island from Ilfracombe, Bideford and Clovelly. ⊗ *Brittany Ferries: Plymouth; 08712 440744; www.brittany-ferries.co.uk • Isles of Scilly Steamship: Quay St, Penzance; 08457 105555, 01736 334220 • Lundy Shore Office: The Quay, Bideford; 01271 863636; www.lundyisland. co.uk*

By Road
The region is connected by a good network of roads, though the elongated shape of the peninsula means that most east-west traffic is concentrated along the A30 and A39 roads.

By Coach
National Express coaches run up to Penzance with stops at Exeter, Plymouth, St Austell, Newquay, Bodmin, Truro, Falmouth, Helston and St Ives. ⊗ *National Express: 08717 818178 • www.nationalexpress.com*

By Local Bus
Local buses are a scenic and cheap way to tour the region. Several companies offer passes for unlimited travel over one, three or seven days. Pick up timetables from tourist offices or stations.

By Train
As well as the main line connecting Exeter, Bodmin, Plymouth, Truro, St Austell and Penzance, branch lines pass through scenic countryside. From Exeter, trains travel south to Exmouth, Torquay and Paignton and north to Barnstaple. From Liskeard, a line heads to Looe. Another crosses to Newquay from Par, and St Erth has a connecting line to St Ives. Call National Rail Enquiries for details. ⊗ *National Rail Enquiries: 08457 484950*

By Organized Excursion
Many companies offer group travel by coach or minibus. These range from backpackers' buses to luxury coaches. Southwest Tourism will give details (see p108).

By Local Ferry
Ferry services across rivers and estuaries often save a big detour. The Kingswear Ferry avoids the long route around the River Dart to reach Dartmouth. Passenger ferries operate between St Mawes and Falmouth, Padstow and Rock and, in summer, between Fowey and Mevagissey.

By Bicycle
You can cycle the whole peninsula. Off-road routes include the Granite Way on Dartmoor, the Camel Trail, the Tarka Trail and the Coast-to-Coast Trail, which connects Portreath on the North Cornish coast to Devoran on the south.

On Foot
Most of the region is great for walking. The South West Coast Path encompasses the whole peninsula on its route. Bodmin Moor, Exmoor and Dartmoor are ideal for inland hikes. Tourist offices can provide itineraries (see p108).

Airports

Exeter International Airport
Map L4
• Clyst Honiton, Exeter
• 01392 367433

Newquay Cornwall Airport
Map C4
• St Mawgan
• 01637 860600

Land's End Airport
Map A5
• Kelynack, St Just
• 08457 105555, 01736 788871

Left **A tourist information centre** Right **Dartmoor National Park information office**

Sources of Information

1 Tourist Information Centres

Every major town – and some villages – has a tourist information centre (TIC), although some are now privately run, with premium rate telephone numbers. Larger offices may also offer an accommodation booking service, either free or for a fee. Most places are open 9am–5pm Monday to Saturday. During summer, many centres stay open on Sundays, while in winter they may have reduced hours or close altogether.
🏵 *Southwest Tourism*
• *www.visitsouthwest.co.uk*

2 National Park Visitor Centres

Dartmoor and Exmoor national parks both have an independent network of visitor centres, which provide useful information services and have books and maps on the area.
🏵 *Dartmoor National Park: Tavistock Road, Princetown; 01822 890414; www.dartmoor-npa.gov.uk*
• *Exmoor National Park: 7–9 Fore Street, Dulverton; 01398 323841; www. exmoor-nationalpark.gov.uk*

3 Websites

All tourist offices have their own local websites. Most hotels, sights and transport companies also have pages where you can book rooms, view information and look up times and timetables.

4 Local Newspapers

Regional newspapers, such as the *Western Morning News* and *West Briton*, usually publish listings for events. They also provide information on local closures, road-works, tide times and the weather. Magazines such as *Inside Cornwall* and *Devon Life* are useful for cultural coverage.

5 Mobile Apps

Resort South West, Cornwall Guide, App for Cornwall, My Devon and Devon Life are extensive and free. Westcountry Beaches lists more than 190 beaches in Devon and Cornwall.

6 Television & Radio

As with the local press, local news broadcasts, TV programmes and the radio provide details about events, traffic and the weather. Surfers in particular will find reports on wind and sea conditions especially useful. Tune in to the BBC's Radio Devon (94.8, 95.8, 103.4 or 104.3 FM) and Radio Cornwall (95.2 or 103.9 FM) and commercial stations such as Gemini FM (96.4, 97 or 103 FM), Plymouth Sound (97 FM) and Atlantic FM (105–107 FM). These stations can be picked up on digital radio (DAB).

7 Weather & Surf Reports

When planning a day out, it is wise to be clued up on the weather forecast. Conditions in the region can change with alarming rapidity and hikers especially can run into danger by being caught unawares. Check the forecast on TV, radio, newspapers, the Internet or at tourist offices. A host of websites supply up-to-date information on sea conditions for surfers. Try www.a1surf.com or magicseaweed.com.

8 Disabled Travellers

Both the National Trust and English Heritage cater for the disabled. Information on wheelchair and mobility scooter hire for disabled travellers can be found on www. accessiblecountryside. org.uk and www. countrysidemobility.org.

9 Listings Magazines

Large towns like Exeter and Plymouth have free listings magazines covering large parts of the region. These can be found at tourist offices, pubs or cafés. *247* is a popular music and lifestyle magazine.

10 Maps

Road maps of Devon and Cornwall are available in bookshops and at newsagents. If you want more detailed maps, the Explorer, Ordnance Survey Landranger, and Outdoor Leisure are recommended. Harvey's maps cover the South West Coast Path and Dartmoor.

www.cornwall.gov.uk and www.devon.gov.uk also give useful information on accessibility in towns and villages.

Left **An ATM in St Mawes** Centre **A traditional red telephone box** Right **A typical post box**

⁀⁑⁂ Banking and Communications

Money
The pound sterling is divided into 100 pence (p). Notes come in denominations of £5, £10, £20 and £50. Coins are 1p, 2p, 5p, 10p, 20p, 50p, £1 and £2.

Banks
Banks are generally open 9:30am–4:30pm Monday to Friday and most have 24-hour external cash machines (ATMs). You can also find ATMs within some food stores and outside supermarkets.

Bureaux de Change
The few independent bureaux de change in Devon and Cornwall are regulated and usually display rates and commission charges. Main post offices change money for no commission. Be sure to compare exchange rates, as these may be unfavourable when commission charges are low.

Credit Cards
Most places accept cards. MasterCard and Visa are common, American Express less so and Diner's Club is rare. B&Bs and smaller campsites may not accept cards, or may ask for a surcharge if they do. Credit cards can be used to withdraw cash from ATMs, but you pay interest from the time of withdrawal.

Postal Services
Post offices are scattered throughout the region, though they may be sparse in rural areas. They open 9am–5:30pm Monday to Friday and 9am–12:30pm or 9am–1pm on Saturdays, with post offices in towns open until 5:30pm. Smaller branches close on Wednesday afternoons. You can buy stamps at newsagents. ◈ *Post office helpline: 08457 223344* • *www.postoffice.co.uk*

Postal Charges
Post offices and the Royal Mail website provide details about postal charges. The rates depend on the size of the package, the destination and time of arrival. For destinations in the UK, letters can be sent first class for next-day delivery or on a cheaper second-class rate for delivery within three working days. Surface mail and express delivery options are also available. ◈ *Royal Mail: 08456 112970* • *www.royalmail.com*

Internet
Most hotels, B&Bs and cafés provide an Internet or Wi-Fi service, sometimes for a fee. Some tourist centres have terminals for public use, though often restricted to a few minutes. Towns such as Exeter and Plymouth have Internet cafés that charge per hour. Public libraries in most towns offer free Internet access, but book in advance. Some phone booths are equipped for email service.

Mobile Phones
Mobiles can be used in most parts of Devon and Cornwall, but some areas are outside signal range, including many coastal and moorland zones. Check before leaving home that your phone works in the UK.

Telephones
Public call boxes found in towns and most villages accept coins (20p minimum) and some take credit cards. It costs at least £2 to make an overseas call, but it is more expensive to call from your hotel. Numbers prefixed by 0800 or 0808 are free, 0845 numbers have local rates and 0870 national rates. 0906 or 0909 numbers cost up to £1.50 per minute. Dial 100 for the operator and 155 for international calls.

Dialling Codes
Omit area codes when calling within the same locality from a land line. When calling from abroad, first dial the access code and then the area code, but omit the initial 0. To call abroad, dial 00 followed by the access code of the country. For directory enquiries, dial 118 500 for domestic and 118 505 for overseas assistance.

Left **Lifeguards on Fistral Beach** Right **Adder, commonly found in the region**

Security and Health

Emergencies
Dial 999 in the event of an emergency. The operator will connect you to the service you need. The call is free from public telephones.

Personal Protection
Provided you follow basic precautions, you are unlikely to encounter any threats. To avoid confrontations with binge drinkers, bypass pubbing areas on Friday and Saturday nights in resorts such as Newquay and Torquay, and in Plymouth, which has a large naval population. Mugging is rare. It is illegal to carry weapons.

Theft
Petty theft can occur in this region. Valuables are best deposited with your hotel, campsite or B&B hosts. Lock your vehicle and lodge it in a protected car park if you are leaving it for any length of time. Beware of pickpockets in shopping areas and on public transport and don't leave your possessions unattended. If a theft occurs, contact the local police to obtain a crime report number to make an insurance claim.
Non-emergency contact for police: 101 (24 hours)

Lost Property
If you lose any property, contact the local police station, or – if it was lost on a bus or train – the transport company you used.

Ticks and Snakes
Ticks can transmit diseases such as Lyme disease. Small and black, these arachnids can attach themselves to you on moorlands and in wooded areas. To avoid picking one up, cover your arms and legs on walks. If you find one on your skin, consult a doctor or pharmacist promptly. Adders with zigzag markings are the only snakes in the region to beware of. Thankfully they are quite rare. If you are bitten by one, seek medical attention.
NHS: 111 • www.nhs.uk

Sea Hazards
Weaver fish can be found on some beaches at low tide. Stepping on them, or on jelly fish, in bare feet can cause painful stings. Take precautions by wearing jelly shoes (plastic sandals). Take care not to be stranded by high tides, which move in quickly, and beware of powerful currents that can sweep you out to sea when you swim. Lifeguards are present on the main beaches, where you are advised to swim between the red and yellow flags.

Hospitals
The hospitals listed below have 24-hour Accident and Emergency departments where you can get treated.
Royal Devon and Exeter Hospital: Barrack Rd, Exeter 01392 411611 • Derriford Hospital: Derriford Rd, Crownhill, Plymouth; 0845 155 8155 • Royal Cornwall Hospital: Treliske, Truro; 01872 250000

Pharmacies
Pharmacies, known as chemists in the UK, are present in every town and large village and can advise on minor ailments. Most are open 9am–5pm Monday to Saturday. Many drugs are only available by prescription from a doctor or hospital. Drugs are known by various names in different countries, so if possible, carry a bottle or packet of the drug that you need.

Dentists
Although there are dentists in most towns, few will accept patients who are not registered. In an emergency, call the dental helpline (01872 354375 in Cornwall and 01392 823348 in Devon).

Women Travellers
There are no inherent problems for female tourists in Devon and Cornwall, though solo travellers should avoid deserted areas at night and not ride in unregistered cabs.

Left **Heavy traffic in Totnes town centre** Right **Hikers on a coastal path near Porthcurno**

Things to Avoid

1 School Holidays, Weekends and Bank Holidays

With its beaches and outdoor activities, the region is popular with families, so the best bathing spots and top sights attract throngs. The summer break – between late July and early September – sees the biggest crowds, the least accommodation and the highest prices. Weekends and bank holidays also get uncomfortably crowded. Expect to queue up to visit sights and restaurants. Hotels and B&Bs often require a minimum of two- or three-nights' stay at weekends.

2 Feeding Seagulls and Ponies

Heed the notices not to feed seagulls, even inadvertently from discarded takeaway containers. Seagulls can get very aggressive, particularly in the nesting season. Eating ice creams or fish and chips by a wall will prevent an attack. It is illegal to feed the ponies on Dartmoor and Bodmin Moor. Besides being unhealthy for them, it encourages them to stray off the moor onto the roads and cause accidents.

3 Driving on Saturdays

Saturday is "changeover day" in the West Country, when people in holiday homes on weekly rentals move into or vacate their property. As a result, roads and trains may be very crowded.

4 Driving in Villages

Many villages are difficult to reach by public transport but with one-way systems and pedestrian areas, they are often tricky to negotiate by car. Fishing villages, especially, cannot handle traffic. Leave your car in a car park, or better still, cycle or walk.

5 Rush Hour

As in every other part of Britain, rush hour can be stressful for drivers and cyclists. In Exeter, Plymouth and Truro, traffic slows completely and country roads too can get congested. Avoid the road between 8 and 9am, and 4:30 and 6pm.

6 Minor Roads at Night

Travelling by road at night not only means you can't admire any scenery that you may pass by, but it can also be dangerous. Coastal roads are often unlit and prone to unexpected twists, while ponies and sheep stray onto unfenced roads.

7 Late Booking of Accommodation

While it may sometimes appear that resorts are full of hotels and B&Bs, availability can be limited during peak times. Campsites and hostels too are booked weeks in advance. Do not count on finding accommodation without a reservation.

8 Saturday-Night Bingers

Devon and Cornwall are no more immune to binge drinking than other parts of Britain. Most places are perfectly calm, but you may come across rowdy behaviour on weekends. Plymouth, Newquay and Torquay are particularly prone to this, though it is quite rare to encounter any violence.

9 Hiking Without Preparation

Any walk longer than a 10-minute stroll should be planned. On the moors and the coasts, the weather can deteriorate quickly; it is not unusual for sunshine to turn to fog without warning. Carry rainproof gear. For longer hikes, carry a map and water, wear stout boots and always inform someone of your route. Remember that often the most scenic areas are out of range of mobile-phone signals.

10 Getting Stranded by Tides

All beaches are liable to be affected by tidal changes. The speed with which a beach can be flooded by high tide is unnerving and it is easy to be cut off from a path back to safety. Take great care wading through fast-moving water.

Left **A harbourside café** Centre **Cycling along the Camel Trail** Right **A town bus in Penzance**

Budget Tips

1 Reduced Admissions

Many museums, galleries and sites such as ruined castles are free; if there is a charge, it is usually reduced for children and senior citizens. Discounts are offered for students and the unemployed on production of a card or document. Family tickets (two adults and two kids) are also available.

2 High Season, Low Season and Weekends

Accommodation rates are often higher in peak season and at weekends. However, hotels that primarily cater to business travellers charge less at weekends. Rates are lowest during winter and places such as gardens, whose allure diminishes during winter, also charge less.

3 Hotels and B&Bs

Bed-and-Breakfasts (B&Bs) are usually cheaper than hotels and offer better value. Rates for "short breaks" (three or four nights) are discounted. Hotels and some B&Bs with dining rooms may offer dinner, bed and breakfast packages that are worth considering.

4 Hostels, Bunkhouses, Campsites and Camping Barns

Hostels belonging to the Youth Hostels Association (YHA) offer good accommodation for a fraction of the price of hotels and most have self-catering kitchens. Other hostels, such as surf lodges, are more spartan. Bunkhouses and camping barns with basic facilities exist in rural areas, but early booking is required as they are often rented to groups. Campsites (usually closed in winter), from farmers' fields to well-equipped complexes, are the cheapest option.

5 Train Travel

The more in advance you book your ticket, the cheaper it will be. Same-day tickets are the most expensive, though return tickets can save a few pounds. Standard tickets cost less than first class. If you plan on frequent train travel, enquire about Rover tickets, which allow unlimited travel over a specific period.

6 Bus and Coach Travel

Buses (for short-distance trips) and coaches (for cross-country runs) are cheaper than trains, but take longer. National Express, the main long-distance coach operator, offers discounted "fun fares" for specific journeys booked in advance *(see p107)*. Megabus also offers cheap fares for journeys between London, Exeter, Plymouth and Newquay. Locally, individual bus companies offer money-saving Explorer tickets. Contact Traveline for details.
- $\circledS$ *Megabus: 09001 600900; www.megabus.com*
- *Traveline: 08712 002233; www.traveline.org.uk*

7 Walking and Biking

The cheapest way to get around is on foot or by bike. The coast path, in particular, is a wonderful resource for travelling by foot. Most train companies carry bikes for free, but some require prior booking; it is worth doing so, as bike-carrying capacity is limited.

8 Eating Out

If you are eating out, you can save a great deal by opting for places offering set-price menus, especially at lunchtime and before 7pm.

9 Self-Catering

Apartment and cottage rentals are usually cheaper than hotels and B&Bs as they offer self-catering facilities. Campsites have washing-up areas, but no kitchens, nor do they encourage open fires for cooking, though barbecues are allowed.

10 Markets

The West Country has markets where you can buy fresh produce at low prices. Clothes are also sold. Enquire about these at the local tourist office *(see p108)*.

Left **A dinghy** Centre **Surfing at Woolacombe Bay** Right **Photographing the coastline**

🔟 Specialist Holidays

Cultural Holidays
You can take in everything from Tudor mansions to art colonies on organized tours lasting a day or stretching over a week. Other interests include field trips to explore the region's archaeological heritage, seafood cookery courses, and painting courses. Accommodation is in places that reflect the subject, such as historic hotels or artist-run B&Bs.

Touring Holidays
Devon and Cornwall offer several attractions that can be sampled on regular coach tours from London, Exeter and Plymouth. With all accommodation arranged for you, you can sit back and enjoy the scenery.

Walking Holidays
Whether on riverside strolls or moorland hikes, walking is one of the main attractions of the West Country. Joining an organized group provides structure, company and expertise in the form of knowledgeable guides. The cheapest and easiest option would be to hook up with the small groups that venture daily onto Dartmoor on circular walks lasting three–six hours. For longer hikes, companies arrange guides and accommodation at select hostels, hotels or B&Bs along the way. Baggage is transported independently.

Cycling Holidays
A network of cycleways allows you to explore the region at your own pace. Operators supply bikes, itineraries and maps and arrange overnight stops. Mountain bikes, bikes for kids, tandems and trailers are all available, as are helmets and child-seats. Favourite routes include Devon's Tarka Trail *(see p36)* and Cornwall's Camel Trail *(see p30)*. Most of the routes are flat, with numerous stops possible at pubs and picnic spots. Bike rental outfits deliver and collect bikes to and from your hotel.

Surfing Holidays
The region has some of Britain's best surfing beaches. Several companies cater to enthusiasts – the majority are in Newquay, the "surf capital". They offer boards, wetsuits and tuition by qualified instructors, and some cater to women-only groups.

Riding Holidays
Dartmoor and Exmoor in particular are popular areas for treks, but stables are scattered across the whole region, with direct access to riding terrain. Rides are for people of all abilities and lessons are available.

YHA Holidays
The Youth Hostels Association (YHA) is the biggest provider of activity holidays. Many of its hostels provide courses over weekends. While most hostels are fully modernized, some offer accommodation in basic camping barns. Many are situated on the coast.
🕲 *Youth Hostels Association* • *01629 592700, 08000 191700* • *www.yha.org.uk*

Sailing Holidays
The more sheltered southern seaboard of Devon and Cornwall is ideal to mess about in boats. Companies based in Dartmouth, Salcombe, Plymouth and Falmouth provide all the know-how you need. You can learn the ropes on basic dinghies or join the crew of a restored sailing ship.

Wildlife Holidays
Devon and Cornwall are a wildlife-lover's haven, offering rich opportunities for anyone interested in hawks, owls, otters or snakes. The estuaries in particular hold some of the nation's rarest species of waders and wildfowl. On sea safaris, you can get close to seals, dolphins and basking sharks.

Adventure Holidays
The region offers action-packed adventure holidays for every taste, either adult-only or for families. Instructors teach basic survival skills on weekend multi-activity courses.

Left **The Scarlet** Centre **Bovey Castle** Right **Hotel Tresanton**

🔟 Luxury Hotels

1 The Scarlet
This much-talked-about eco hotel is embedded into the cliffs above Mawgan Porth beach. It boasts a luxurious spa, chic restaurant, reed-cleaned pool and log-fired hot tubs, some with spectacular views. ❧ Map C4 • Tredragon Rd, Mawgan Porth • 01637 861800 • www.scarlet hotel.co.uk • £££££

2 South Sands Hotel
Waves practically lap right up to this New England-style, contemporary hotel. It has a grand spiral staircase and an excellent restaurant. The blue and white theme with nautical touches runs throughout the 22 bedrooms. ❧ Map J6 • Bolt Head, Salcombe • 01548 859000 • www. southsands.com • £££££

3 Burgh Island Hotel
This palatial structure set on its own island is a testament to Art Deco elegance. Its curves and turret give it the appearance of an oceanliner, while the interior is reminiscent of the Jazz Age. Facilities include a rock pool and helipad. ❧ Map J6 • Bigbury-on-Sea, Devon • 01548 810514 • www. burghisland.com • £££££

4 Hotel Tresanton
An ex-yachting club, this hotel has rooms decorated with Cornish art, most offering panoramic views over the Carrick Roads Estuary. There is a cinema and an Italian-inspired restaurant here. Guests can use the yacht and speedboat in summer. ❧ Map C5 • 27 Lower Castle Rd, St Mawes • 01326 270055 • www.tresanton.com • £££££

5 Combe House
Country house elegance does not come any better than this. The tone is more intimate than formal, and the bedrooms are plush. The outstanding restaurant serves wines from the manor house's underground cellars (see p43). ❧ Map L3 • Gittisham, Devon • 01404 540400 • www.combehousedevon. co.uk • £££££

6 Gidleigh Park
This romantic haven at the end of a narrow lane in Dartmoor, has traditional rooms decorated with antiques and equipped with modern gadgetry. The restaurant is one of the region's best (see p81). ❧ Map J4 • Chagford, Devon • 01647 432367 • www. gidleigh.co.uk • £££££

7 Hotel Endsleigh
A former hunting lodge transformed into an island of opulence by the team responsible for the Tresanton. Each of the 16 rooms is different, but all have been restored to their Georgian appearance. A stretch of the River Tamar runs through the estate. ❧ Map H4 • Milton Abbot, Tavistock • 01822 870000 • www.hotelendsleigh.com • £££££

8 Lewtrenchard Manor
This secluded Jacobean manor house boasts oak-panelled rooms, stone fireplaces and sleigh beds in the bedrooms. The restaurant uses ingredients from home-grown produce to prepare meals. ❧ Map H3 • Lewdown, Okehampton • 01566 783222 • www. lewtrenchard.co.uk • ££££

9 Bovey Castle
Surrounded by majestic parkland, this mansion has stately, well-equipped rooms. Activities include tennis, a spa and an 18-hole golf course. The afternoon tea is recommended. ❧ Map K4 • North Bovey, Dartmoor, Devon • 01647 445000, 08444 740077 • www. boveycastle.com • £££££

10 Hell Bay
Situated in a secluded cove on Bryher, the smallest of the Scilly islands, this hotel offers the ultimate escape. The rooms have stunning views and artworks by famous Cornish artists. There is an outdoor pool and spa treatments as well. ❧ Map A4 • Bryher, Isles of Scilly • 01720 422947 • www.hellbay. co.uk • £££££

Gurnard's Head

Price Categories

For a standard double room per night, inclusive of taxes and any additional charges.

£ under £65
££ £65–£100
£££ £100–£150
££££ £150–£200
£££££ over £200

🔟 Seaside Hotels

The Slipway Hotel
There is a real sense of getting away from it all in this quayside hotel in a typical Cornish village. Some of the rooms look out onto the water, just a stone's throw away. The hotel has a good restaurant and a cheerful bar. Parking is some way up the hill. ⊗ Map D3 • Harbour Front, Port Isaac • 01208 880264 • www. portisaachotel.com • £££

Gurnard's Head
The seven rooms of this inn are simply furnished and have feathery-soft beds. Stripped floors and open fires add to the ambience. There is not a lot of space but the setting is spectacular and the food in the restaurant is heavenly (see p103). ⊗ Map A5 • Zennor, Cornwall • 01736 796928 • www.gurnards head.co.uk • £££

The Red Lion
Dominating Clovelly's small harbour, the antique Red Lion hotel has a nautical flavour. The rooms, though small, have wonderful sea or harbour views. Guests can use a lane at the back of this traffic-free village to reach the hotel. ⊗ Map G2 • Clovelly • 01237 431237 • www. clovelly.co.uk • ££

The Old Quay House
Truly the lap of luxury, this hotel is located overlooking the water-front, with big windows and a sun terrace taking advantage of the vista. Rooms are opulent – those with river views cost more. The restaurant is one of Cornwall's best. ⊗ Map E4 • 28 Fore St, Fowey • 01726 833302 • No under-12s • www.the oldquayhouse.com • ££££

Driftwood Spars
Relics from ship-wrecks went into the construction of this 17th-century building. Most of the rooms offer sea or garden views. One of the hotel's three bars has live music at weekends. ⊗ Map C4 • Trevaunance Cove, St Agnes, Cornwall • 01872 552428 • www. driftwoodspars.com • ££

Saunton Sands Hotel
The stunning location above the beach is the biggest draw of this cliff-top hotel. There are indoor and outdoor pools, tennis courts and country paths for excursions. Insist on a room facing the sea. ⊗ Map H1 • Braunton, Devon • 01271 890212 • www.saunton sands.co.uk • £££££

Pier House Hotel
Superbly positioned on the quayside, this hotel offers comfort and charm. There is a bistro and a formal restaurant serving delicious food and a pub next door. The South West Coast Path passes directly outside and the Eden Project (see pp10–11) is only a few minutes' drive away. ⊗ Map D4 • Charlestown, St Austell, Cornwall • 01726 67955 • www.pierhouse hotel.com • £££

Fistral Beach Hotel and Spa
Located on Fistral, Cornwall's premier surf beach, this contemporary four-star hotel offers great sea views from many of its rooms. Facilities include a spa, pool and fitness suite. ⊗ Map C4 • Esplanade Rd, Newquay, Cornwall • 01637 852221 • www.fistral beachhotel.co.uk • £££

Imperial Hotel
This stately pile on a height above the sea exudes splendour, with its chandeliers, marble floors and a formal ambience. Bedrooms are spacious – it is worth paying extra for a front-facing one with a superb view. ⊗ Map K5 • Park Hill Rd, Torquay • 01803 294301 • www.the hotelcollection.co.uk • ££

Primrose Valley Hotel
An independent boutique hotel, Primrose Valley is just off the picturesque, white-sand Porthminster Beach. It has an environ-mentally friendly ethos and individually decorated rooms. ⊗ Map B5 • Porthminster Beach, St Ives • 01736 794939 • www. primroseonline.co.uk • £££

Left **Abbey Hotel** Centre **Southernay House** Right **Royal Seven Stars Hotel**

TOP 10 Town Hotels

1 Abbey Hotel
Antiques, books and smouldering fires make this 17th-century hotel a real find. A few rooms at this colourful, chic place have superb views over St Michael's Mount. ◈ *Map B5 • Abbey St, Penzance • 01736 366906 • www.theabbeyonline. co.uk • £££*

2 Yeo Dale Hotel
Some rooms are grand and some are more basic, but all are beautifully decorated in this friendly Georgian hotel, close to the centre of Barnstaple. The dining room enjoys a view over the River Yeo. ◈ *Map H2 • Pilton Bridge, Barnstaple • 01271 342954 • www. yeodalehotel.co.uk • ££*

3 Browns Hotel
Sophisticated Browns Hotel has elegant rooms, modern art on the walls and a clubby atmosphere. Breakfast includes orange juice and a wide range of teas, while the restaurant serves evening meals and tapas throughout the day. ◈ *Map K6 • 27–9 Victoria Rd, Dartmouth • 01803 832572 • www.browns hoteldartmouth.co.uk • £££*

4 Royal Seven Stars Hotel
This atmospheric coaching inn in the centre of Totnes has been modernized but retains its 17th-century charm. The contemporary rooms come with en-suite showers. The hotel has a restaurant and two bars serving snacks. ◈ *Map K5 • The Plains, Totnes • 01803 862125 • www.royalseven stars.co.uk • £££*

5 Mannings Hotel
This central hostelry has a contemporary feel and is ideal for a night or two in Cornwall's capital. The rooms are individually designed and apartments are also available. The bar and grill serves Mediterranean-style food. ◈ *Map C5 • Lemon St, Truro • 01872 270345 • www.mannings hotels.co.uk • £££*

6 Abode Exeter
Locally known as the Royal Clarence, one of the country's oldest hotels has been modernized and boasts fully equipped rooms. Its main draw is its location opposite Exeter Cathedral and the Michael Caines restaurant (see p81). ◈ *Map P2 • Cathedral Yard, Exeter • 01392 319955 • www. abodeexeter.co.uk • £££*

7 Greenbank Hotel
Overlooking the scenic Fal estuary, the Greenbank is just a few minutes' walk from the centre of Falmouth. Many of the rooms offer great views of the river and all guests have access to the wonderful waterside terrace. The restaurant uses the best of Cornish produce, including locally caught seafood. ◈ *Map C5 • Harbourside, Falmouth • 01326 312440 • www.greenbank-hotel. co.uk • ££££*

8 Southernay House
An upmarket boutique hotel in the business quarter of Exeter, Southernay House is a blend of classic styling and modern comforts. Occupying a Grade II-listed townhouse, it has ten bedrooms, a restaurant, a bar and a private dining room. ◈ *Map K3 • 36 Southernay East, Exeter • 01392 439000 • www. southernayhouse.com • ££££*

9 Browns
Located on the edge of Dartmoor, this coaching inn has been refashioned into a boutique hotel and has a brasserie, courtyard and conservatory. The elegant rooms have the latest gadgetry. ◈ *Map H4 • 80 West St, Tavistock • 01822 618686 • www. brownsdevon.com • £££*

10 Bowling Green Hotel
This hotel next to Plymouth Hoe has comfortable beds in good-sized rooms. The tasty breakfast will set you up for the day. Secure parking is a bonus in Plymouth. ◈ *Map P6 • 9–10 Osborne Place, Lockyer St, The Hoe, Plymouth • 01752 209090 • www.bowlinggreenhotel. com • ££*

Price Categories

For a standard double room per night, inclusive of taxes and any additional charges.

£	under £65
££	£65–£100
£££	£100–£150
££££	£150–£200
£££££	over £200

Mason's Arms

🔟 Budget Hotels and B&Bs

1 The Old Rectory
This rural guesthouse on Boscastle's outskirts was the place where author Thomas Hardy stayed. All rooms are preserved in their Victorian splendour and there are lovely wooded gardens. ✪ *Map D2 • St Juliot, Boscastle • 01840 250225 • Closed Dec–mid-Feb • No under-12s • www.stjuliot.com • ££*

2 East Dyke Farmhouse
A 15-minute walk above the honeypot of Clovelly, this 200-year-old farmhouse has three spacious bedrooms equipped with fridges and private bathrooms. There is a flagstoned dining room for hearty breakfasts served around a large table. ✪ *Map G2 • Higher Clovelly, Devon • 01237 431216 • No credit cards • £*

3 The Hollies Guest House
Hosts, Mike and Pam Fletcher take pride in looking after their guests in their Regency house, just a short walk from the seafront. Spacious rooms, a garden and superb breakfasts make this a great place to stay. ✪ *Map L4 • Salcombe Rd, Sidmouth • 01395 514580 • www.holliesguesthouse.co.uk • £*

4 Mount Tavy Cottage
This B&B set in a lush garden is a great base for walkers. Guests can sleep in a 250-year-old gardener's cottage or in two garden studios. Generous breakfasts are served and evening meals are available by prior arrangement. Bring your own wine. Self-catering accommodation is also offered. ✪ *Map H4 • Tavistock, Devon • 01822 614253 • www.mounttavy.co.uk • ££*

5 Sixteen
Expect a warm welcome at this terraced house which is a mix of the antique and the contemporary. Inside, it is decorated with art by students of Falmouth College of Art and outside there is a sunny deck and a garden. ✪ *Map C5 • 16, Western Terrace, Falmouth • 01326 319920 • No credit cards • www.sixteen falmouth.co.uk • ££*

6 Treverbyn House
This Edwardian guesthouse up from Padstow's harbour has spacious rooms with open fires and wooden or cast-iron beds. Breakfast is served in the room or on a terrace with river views. Parking is available. ✪ *Map D3 • Station Rd, Padstow • 01841 532855 • No credit cards • www.treverbynhouse.com • £££*

7 Zennor Chapel
This old Methodist chapel, located in the village where D H Lawrence once lived, has five comfortable rooms and is close to the South West Coast Path. There is a café serving home-made food attached, plus a gift shop. There's a regular bus service to St Ives ✪ *Map A5 • Zennor, St Ives • 01736 798307 • www.zennorchapel guesthouse.com • ££*

8 Venton Vean
A beautifully renovated townhouse, Venton Vean offers three plush B&B bedrooms and plenty of luxuries such as goose-down duvets and excellent breakfasts, including Mexican or Spanish choices. ✪ *Map B5 • Trewithen Rd, Penzance • 01736 351294 • www.ventonvean.co.uk • ££*

9 Mason's Arms
One of the prettiest villages in East Devon boasts this exceptional inn. The traditional rooms range from the grand, with beamed ceilings, to smaller options. The food is gourmet and the setting idyllic. ✪ *Map L4 • Branscombe • 01297 680300 • www.masons arms.co.uk • ££*

10 Tregarthen Guest House
This welcoming and modern B&B has seven rooms, is a 10-minute walk to the centre of town, and provides hearty breakfasts. ✪ *Map C4 • 1 Arundel Way, Newquay • 01637 873554 • www.tregarthen.co.uk • £*

Left **Boscastle YHA** Centre **Lizard YHA** Right **Falmouth Lodge**

Hostels and Bunkhouses

1 Sparrowhawk Backpackers

Well-placed for excursions to Dartmoor, this hostel has dormitories in a converted stable and double rooms in the main house. A large kitchen is on site and you can order organic vegetables in advance. Pubs and restaurants are a brief stroll up the street.
◉ *Map J4* • *45 Ford St, Moretonhampstead* • *01647 440318* • *www.sparrowhawk backpackers.co.uk* • *£££*

2 Falmouth Lodge

This scrupulously tidy hostel down a quiet street is close to the railway station. There is a TV lounge, well-equipped kitchen and dining room. Bunkrooms and private rooms are available.
◉ *Map C5* • *9 Gyllyngvase Terrace, Falmouth* • *01326 319996* • *www.falmouth backpackers.co.uk* • *££££*

3 Lizard YHA

Located on Britain's most southerly point, the Lizard YHA is one of the best YHA hostels in England. Choose between dormitory rooms or bigger family rooms, many with sea views.◉ *Map C6* • *Lizard Point, Cornwall* • *0845 3719550* • *Open Apr–Oct* • *www. yha.org.uk* • *££££*

4 Boscastle YHA

This hostel on Boscastle's quayside was all but washed away during a flash flood in 2004. Now restored, it provides excellent accommodation in one of Cornwall's loveliest spots, with coast walks on either side. You can sleep in the small dormitories or the family rooms.
◉ *Map D2* • *Palace Stables, Boscastle* • *0845 3719006* • *Open Apr–early-Nov* • *www.yha.org.uk* • *££££*

5 Okehampton YHA

Housed in a converted railway goods shed on the northern edge of Dartmoor, this hostel caters to a gamut of pursuits including rock climbing, gorge scrambling, pony trekking and high ropes. Camping is also possible. ◉ *Map H3* • *Klondyke Rd, Okehampton* • *0845 3719651* • *www. yha.org.uk* • *££££*

6 Penzance YHA

This well-equipped and imposing Georgian mansion, set in beautiful grounds, is a 15-minute walk from the centre of Penzance and open all year. It has a self-catering kitchen, dining room, bunks, double rooms and spacious family rooms, with the option to camp.
◉ *Map B5* • *Castle Horneck, Penzance* • *08453 719653* • *www.yha.org.uk/ hostel/penzance* • *££££*

7 Plume of Feathers

Located at the heart of Dartmoor, this pub occupies the oldest building in Princetown. It runs a couple of bunkhouses with cooking facilities, showers and a day room. Other options include B&B or camping.
◉ *Map J4* • *Princetown, Dartmoor* • *01822 890240* • *www.theplumeoffeathers dartmoor.co.uk* • *£££*

8 Runnage Farm

This cattle and sheep farm near Bellever Forest offers the choice of sleeping in camping barns on raised wooden areas, bunkrooms or camping. A kitchen and showers are provided. Bunk rooms not available at weekends.
◉ *Map J4* • *Postbridge, Yelverton* • *01822 880222* • *www.runnagecamping barns.co.uk* • *£*

9 Navy Blue Lodge

Close to the centre of Newquay and beaches, this small upmarket lodge offers two dormitories for six, a double bedroom and a family room; continental breakfast is included. A two-day minimum stay is essential. ◉ *Map C4* • *45 Pargolla Road, Newquay* • *01637 859156* • *www. navybluelodge.co.uk* • *£££££*

10 North Shore

Surfers make a beeline for this hostel with 11 rooms including en-suite doubles. There is a kitchen for self-catering and barbecues in summer. Internet facilities are available. Doubles cost more. ◉ *Map E2* • *57 Killerton Rd, Bude* • *01288 354256* • *www. northshore bude.com* • *££*

Book ahead for weekends in summer.

Price Categories

For a dormitory bed or a standard camping unit for two people and a pitch.

£	under £10
££	£10–£15
£££	£15–£20
££££	£20–£25
£££££	over £25

Ayr Holiday Park

📖10 Campsites

Ayr Holiday Park
The only campsite in St Ives situated above Porthmeor Beach has terrific sea views. It is pricey but clean and has a solar-powered shower block. The town centre is just a kilometre (half a mile) away. 🔇 *Map B5* • *Ayr Terrace, St Ives* • *01736 795855* • *www. ayrholidaypark.co.uk* • *££££*

Little Meadow
This campsite is located on one of the most scenic stretches of coast in North Devon. Facilities are minimal but include a modern shower block. Footpaths lead to the beach and Watermouth Castle. 🔇 *Map H1* • *Watermouth, Ilfracombe* • *01271 866862* • *Closed Oct–Mar* • *www. little meadow.co.uk* • *££££*

Carnon Downs
One of the few options open all year, this large site between Truro and Falmouth is sheltered. Though much of the space is given to motor homes, the facilities are excellent and pubs are within walking distance. 🔇 *Map C5* • *Carnon Downs, Truro* • *01872 862283* • *www.carnon-downs-caravanpark.co.uk* • *£££££*

Dennis Cove
Simplicity is the keynote at Dennis Cove, situated alongside the Camel Estuary. The location above the Camel Trail makes it a useful base for anyone wanting to explore this walking and biking route. 🔇 *Map D3* • *Dennis Lane, Padstow* • *01841 532349* • *Closed Oct–Mar* • *www.dennis covecampsite.co.uk* • *££££*

Bryher Campsite
You cannot get much further off the beaten track than at this stripped-down site on the Isles of Scilly. The island views are magnificent. The Fraggle Rock café-pub is close by. 🔇 *Map A4* • *Bryher, Isles of Scilly* • *01720 422559* • *Closed Oct–Mar* • *www.bryhercampsite. co.uk* • *£££*

Cornish Tipi Holidays
This secluded woodland site, close to the north Cornish coast, offers 40 American-style tipis. There is a lake for fishing and fire pits to cook on, but no electricity, although hot showers and flushing toilets are available. You can pay a premium for extra privacy. 🔇 *Map D3* • *Tregeare, Pendoggett, St Kew* • *01208 880781* • *Closed Nov–Mar* • *www. cornishtipiholidays.co.uk* • *£££££*

North Morte Farm
Close to Devon's top surfing beaches, this hilly site is not very sheltered, but has knock-out views over to Lundy. A footpath leads down to a rocky beach while the lovely Woolacombe beach is a 2-km (1-mile) walk away. As it is an extensive site, it very rarely seems overcrowded. 🔇 *Map H1* • *North Morte Rd, Mortehoe, Woolacombe* • *01271 870381* • *Closed Oct–mid-Mar* • *www. northmortefarm.co.uk* • *£££*

Broad Meadow House
This peaceful coastal site offers tents and breakfast for up to 12 people in either a pre-pitched or your own tent. Electricity and hot showers are available. 🔇 *Map D4* • *Quay Rd, Charlestown, St Austell* • *01726 76636* • *Closed Oct–Mar* • *No credit cards* • *www.broadmeadowhouse. com* • *£££££*

Lundy Island Campsite
One of the country's most remote campsites with modern facilities. Diving and climbing are among the activities to be pursued on the island. 🔇 *Map G1* • *Lundy, Devon* • *01271 863636* • *Closed Nov–Mar* • *www.lundy island.co.uk* • *££££*

South Penquite
On the outskirts of Bodmin Moor, this eco-friendly site has spacious pitches and four Mongolian *yurts*. Futons provide comfort, but you have to bring your own sheets. 🔇 *Map E3* • *Blisland* • *01208 850491* • *Closed Nov–Apr* • *www. southpenquite.co.uk* • *££*

General Index

Acknowledgments

The Author

Robert Andrews has been travelling and writing travel guidebooks for 20 years. His main areas of interest are the West Country in England and southern Italy. Based in Bristol, he also writes articles, compiles anthologies and takes photographs.

Publisher
Douglas Amrine

List Manager
Christine Stroyan

Managing Art Editor
Mabel Chan

Senior Editor
Sadie Smith

Senior Designer
Paul Jackson

Project Editor
Ros Walford

Senior Cartographic Editor
Casper Morris

Picture Researcher
Ellen Root

DTP Operator
Natasha Lu

Production Controller
Rita Sinha

Photographer
Nigel Hicks

Additional Photography
Nigel Hicks; Rough Guides/ Tim Draper

Fact Checker
Kate Hughes

Maps
Maps by JP Map Graphics Ltd. based on data from the People's Map.

Revisions Team
Emma Anacootee, Ismay Atkins, Marta Bescos Sanchez, Dipika Dasgupta, Caroline Elliker, Mohammad Hassan, Kaberi Hazarika, Integrated Publishing Solutions, Bharti Karakoti, Sumita Khatwani, Shikha Kulkarni, Priyanka Kumar, Alison McGill, Sonal Modha, Catherine Palmi, Ajay Verma, Debra Wolter.

Picture Credits
a-above; b-below/bottom; c-centre; f-far; l-left; r-right; t-top.

Works of art have been reproduced with the kind permission of the following copyright holders: Barbara Hepworth Sculpture Garden with *Four Square (Walk Through)* 1966 © Bowness, Hepworth Estate 97tr.

The Publisher would like to thank the following individuals, companies and picture libraries for their kind permissions to reproduce their photographs:

THE ABBEY HOTEL: 116tl; ABODE HOTELS: 81tl; ALAMY: Peter Barritt 23tl; Andrew Besley 6cl; David Chapman 8cb, 8br; Patrick Eden 26-7c; geophotos 34tr; Glenn Harper 34bc; Paul Heinrich 38tl; Graham Lawrence 38tr; Christopher Kingswood 109tc; Mary Evans Picture Library 56tr; National Trust Photolibrary/Derek Croucher 8cl; National Trust Photolibrary/Andreas von Einsiedel 9cr; National Trust Photolibrary/John Hammond 8tr; National Trust Photolibrary/Derek Harris 9bc; National Trust Photolibrary/Claire Takacs 50b; National Trust Photolibrary/Geraint Tellem 56bl; Pontino 35tl; The Print Collector 56c.

THE CHARLOTTE TEA HOUSE: 42b; CORBIS: Robert Harding World Imagery/Guy Edwards 79tr; Rune Hellestad 11tl; E.O. Hoppe 56tl; Hulton-Deutsch Collection 57tl; Skyscan 28-9c. DREAMSTIME. COM: Gordon Bell 79tl.

FIFTEEN CORNWALL: Bob Berry 104–5. GETTY IMAGES: Redferns/Caitlin Mogridge 11tl.

DEVON GUILD OF CRAFTSMEN: 60bl; THE DWELLING HOUSE: 42b.

LIZARD LIGHTHOUSE CENTRE: 53tr.

NATIONAL MARITIME MUSEUM CORNWALL: 55tl; NATIONAL TRUST PHOTOLIBRARY: John Bethell 29bl; Andreas von Einsiedel 9tc, 14crb; Jerry Harpur 8-9c. NIGEL HICKS: 7tl, 22cl, 22cb, 22crb 22-3c, 23bl, 23cr. ©NTPL: Andrew Butler 48tl.

PHOTOLIBRARY: Peter Barritt 32-3; David Noton Photography 88-9; Robert Harding Travel 4-5; Thomas Dobner-Dartmoor Collection 72-3. PORTHMEOR BEACH CAFÉ: 102tr.

ROYAL ALBERT MEMORIAL MUSEUM: 19bc.

SEAFOOD RESTAURANT GROUP: 42tr; SOUTHERNAY HOUSE LIMITED: 116tc; THE SCARLET HOTEL: 114tl.

TATE ST IVES: Barbara Hepworth Sculpture Garden Photo © Bob Berry 97tr; THE TINNERS ARMS: 59tl.

All other images are © Dorling Kindersley London. For further information see www.dkimages.com

Selected Town Index